The Yorkshire Terrier

POPULAR DOGS' BREED SERIES

THE
YORKSHIRE
TERRIER

ETHEL MUNDAY

Revised by Vera Munday

POPULAR DOGS
London   Melbourne   Auckland   Johannesburg

Popular Dogs Publishing Co. Ltd

An imprint of Century Hutchinson Ltd

Brookmount House, 62–65 Chandos Place,
Covent Garden, London WC2N 4NW

Century Hutchinson Australia (Pty) Ltd
PO Box 496, 16–22 Church Street, Hawthorn,
Melbourne, Victoria 3122

Century Hutchinson New Zealand Limited
191 Archers Road, PO Box 40–086, Glenfield, Auckland 10

Century Hutchinson South Africa (Pty) Ltd
PO Box 337, Bergvlei 2012, South Africa

First published (as the Popular Yorkshire Terrier) 1958
Revised edition 1962
Revised edition (as The Yorkshire Terrier) 1966, 1968,
1971, 1974, 1976, 1978, 1987

Set in Baskerville by BookEns, Saffron Walden, Essex

Printed and bound by Anchor Brendon Ltd,
Tiptree, Essex

British Library Cataloguing in Publication Data

Munday, Ethel
    The Yorkshire terrier. 9th ed., rev.
    (Popular Dogs' breed series).
    1. Yorkshire terriers
    I. Title   II. Munday, Vera
    636.7'6   SF429.Y6

ISBN 0 09 171240 8

CONTENTS

ILLUSTRATIONS

between pages 48 and 49

Ch. Luna Star of Yadnum
Bred and owned by the author

Ch. Pretty Debbie of Yadnum
Bred by Mrs G. Bulgin. Owned by Miss Vera Munday

Huddersfield Ben
Bred by Mr Eastwood. Owned by Mr J. Kershaw

Ted
Bred and owned by Mrs M. A. Foster

Overdale Marquis
Breeder and owner not known

Ch. Harringay Remarkable
Bred and owned by Mrs Clenshaw

Ch. James Soham
Bred and owned by The Lady Elizabeth Windham

The author with Ch. Midnight Gold and Emperor of Yadnum
Emperor, Midnight Gold and Timothy of Yadnum
Ch. Elmslade Galahad of Yadnum and Ch. Golden Button of Yadnum
Elmslade Galahad: bred by Mrs M. Slade. Owned by the author
Golden Button: bred and owned by the author

between pages 80 and 81

Ch. Deebees Gold Penny
Bred and owned by Mrs S. D. Beech

Ch. Yorkfold Wrupert Bear
Bred and owned by Mrs D. Hillman

Ch. Maritoys Midnight Rose
Bred by Mrs M. Watton. Owned by Mrs J. M. Blaimires

Ch. Wykebank Tinkerbelle
Bred and owned by Mr A. Blaimires

Ch. Shianda Royal Fanfare
Bred and owned by Mr and Mrs G. Davies

Ch. Naylenor Magic Moment
Bred and owned by Mr P. Naylor

A bowlful of puppies

Ch. Azurene Corduroy of Yadnum
Bred by Mrs I. G. Bulgin. Owned by Miss Vera Munday

between pages 112 and 113

Int. Ch. Mr Pimm of Johnstounburn
Bred by Mr G. Brown. Owned by Mrs Crookshank

A 'Yorkie' with his coat tied up

Six Johnstounburn champions

Ch. Robina Gay of Yadnum
Bred and owned by Miss Vera Munday

Ch. Blairsville Royal Seal
Bred and owned by Mr and Mrs Brian Lister

Ch. Yadnum Regal Fare
Bred and owned by Miss Vera Munday

Ch. Polliam Sweet Delight
Bred and owned by Mrs P. Osborne

Ch. Candytops Royal Cascade
Bred and owned by Mr and Mrs E. H. Oakley

Ch. Candytops Strawberry Fare
Bred and owned by Mr and Mrs E. H. Oakley

Illustrations

IN THE TEXT

AUTHOR'S INTRODUCTIONS

My main object in writing this book has been to try to pass on to the novice much of the knowledge I have gained as a breeder of Yorkshire Terriers through the years, together with kindly advice from many friends who are also successful breeders and exhibitors, and to help identify the qualities of the breed, be it a show dog or purely a pet, with as little effort as possible.

As a matter of interest I have given a few facts relating to the history and origin of the breed, and I have added some information regarding the treatment of the Yorkshire in health and sickness.

This little dog has a surprisingly independent character, will amuse himself, and makes few demands on his owner apart from his feeding, exercise, and attention to toilet. Given these three essentials he enjoys good health, lives a long life, and asks little from his owner, but what he has to *give* would take more than one book to write about.

In this book I have tried to help the breeder to realize the desirability of building up a strain of his own. To be the owner of many successful generations, all from the same stock, is most gratifying, for physical features and traits of character are an ever-astonishing source of wonderment.

My thanks are due to the friends who provided material for illustrations, and my only regret is that not all the photographs would stand reproduction. I must emphasize the great value of these illustrations, for as historical records I feel they can contribute much towards the advancement of the breed. Excluding a few, the dogs they portray have all reached top honours.

Although I have owned Yorkshire Terriers for over forty years there is always more to be learned about them and if any

9

noticeable omissions have been made I ask the reader's
forgiveness.
1958

Since its first publication eight years ago I have received letters
about this book from many countries. It is good to know that
the attractive little Yorkie has so many friends the world over,
and I am sure that he will continue to endear himself to dog
lovers. The appendices of the present third edition, now
republished under the title of *The Yorkshire Terrier*, have again
been revised and brought up-to-date.
1966

I was delighted to hear that this book was going into a fourth
edition. The Yorkie continues to increase in popularity, and in
1967 it was the top export breed from the U.K. This edition
has been brought up-to-date in line with other reprints.
1968

Yet another edition—again brought up-to-date. When I first
wrote this book I could not forecast the great number of letters
I would receive and the number of friends I would make, all
over the world, for just having written about my favourite
breed. The Yorkshire Terrier continues as one of the most
popular breeds of dog of the present day.
1971

Three editions in five years have brought even more friends
from all corners of the world. The text and appendices of this
sixth edition have once more been revised and six of the
photographs have been replaced.
1974

For the seventh edition I have again made a few minor
revisions to the text, brought the appendices up-to-date, and
also added two photographs. The Yorkshire Terrier is now the
most popular breed in the UK, and it is my hope that this book
will continue to be of some assistance to all lovers of the
Yorkie.

1976   E. M.

REVISER'S NOTE

My mother died in August 1977 nearly a year after the seventh edition of her book appeared. She had devoted a lifetime to the Yorkshire Terrier, and the regular reprints of her book on the breed always delighted her. She also derived great pleasure from the many letters written to her as a result of the book and from the many friends which it made her since its first publication twenty years ago.

It was my mother's wish that I should take over responsibility for *The Yorkshire Terrier* and the eighth edition contained a few minor corrections and revisions. This ninth edition has been further revised to bring it up-to-date in accordance with present day requirements, and alterations to parts of the text and additions have been made. I hope that these will help the reader to care for their Yorkshire Terrier.

1988   V.M.

1
Origin

The true origin of the beautiful, fearless, diminutive dog that we know as the Yorkshire Terrier is not really known. In 1874, in the *Kennel Club Stud Book* (first volume), he was classified as 'Broken-haired Scotch Terrier or Yorkshire Terrier', but a few years later, because the breed had been so improved in the county of Yorkshire by authority of the Kennel Club, it was scheduled at shows as the 'Yorkshire Terrier'.

It is doubtful if many of the early Yorkshire Terriers could be traced back to common ancestors, for in an area that knew so many terriers and toy dogs it would be unreasonable to suppose that all breeders used the same crosses.

The Clydesdale or Paisley Terrier must surely play a large part in the make-up of the Yorkshire Terrier. This extinct breed resembled the Skye Terrier in nearly all respects but was shorter in the back; his height was thirteen to fourteen inches from the ground and his weight about 16 lb. The colour of the body coat was a fine dark blue, silky in texture and about five to six inches in length. He was known to have erect ears.

The Broken-haired Scotch Terrier probably played a part in the development of the Yorkshire: one type was a sandy-red colour and carried a shaggy coat; another type had harsh hair, a short muzzle, shortness and stoutness of limb, and was generally a dirty white in colour; another was smooth, sleek, and usually black-and-tan in colour. The mixture of the black-and-tan and white coat of this Scottish breed may account for the white hairs sometimes found on the chest and paws of Yorkshire puppies when born. This is usually replaced by lovely golden-tan hair. It has been noted that a puppy with white hair on the chest invariably carries a lovely coat.

Some think that the Maltese Terrier played a part in this touch of white, but I am not so sure since the Scottish or Broken-haired Terrier seems to be the foundation of many of the long-coated dogs of Scotland and Northern England.

It is also recorded that some hundreds of years ago a breed of terrier with a rough coat lived in the Western Highlands of Scotland and the Hebrides. He was the working type and from him several different types were evolved, probably the result of personal preferences. The Macdonalds of Skye preferred the longer-coated and longer-bodied dogs which are recorded as Skye Terriers. They resemble the Yorkshire Terrier very closely except, of course, for the much longer back, which was developed for hunting out the badger. The Skye Terrier is, of course, four to six times the weight of a Yorkshire Terrier. The colours of the coat are blue-grey with fawn or cream. Perhaps the one breed that was found most suitable to complement the qualities of the Skye Terrier was the Black-and-Tan, or Manchester, Terrier, whose colouring has long been dominant in the Yorkshire.

A very old fancier, John Richardson of Halifax, who was born in the Waterloo decade, traced the Yorkshire Terrier back to the Waterside Terrier, which was common in Yorkshire in the days of King William IV and recorded as a game little animal, occasionally grizzle in colour, weight about 6 lb., with a coat from four to five inches in length and having a silver head.

In the first and second editions of Stonehenge's authoritative *Dogs of the British Isles* there is a plate in which, in addition to a white, broken-haired terrier, there is a dog which is taken as representative of the Yorkshire Terrier. Stonehenge was writing of the usual run of rough terriers to be seen in 1868, and says of this dog: 'Sometimes his coat is of a silky texture and in this case the colours are blue-fawn or blue-tan.'

A writer in *Dogs of the British Isles*, published in 1872, describes the Yorkshire Terrier as

'a silky-coated terrier and with the exception of the colouring and texture of coat, resembles the old English rough terrier, the shape of the body and head being exactly the same. The ears are generally cropped, but if entire should be fine, thin, and moderately small. The coat should be long, very silky in texture, and completely parted down the back, the beard being often two to three inches in length and entirely golden tan. The colour must be entirely blue on the back, and down to the elbows and thigh should be rich lustre and without any mixture of tan. Legs and muzzle should be rich golden tan, ears also tan, but darker in shade. The colour on the top of the skull being lighter, approaching fawn, the two shades gradually merging into each other. Weight, ten to eighteen pounds.'

How closely this description tallies with the present-day Yorkshire except for weight!

At the turn of the century, in the *Dog Book*, James Watson stated that sixty years was as far as we could go back in Yorkshire Terrier pedigrees, when we come to Swift's Old Crab and Kershaw's Old Kitty. The former was a long-coated black-and-tan terrier and the latter a drop-eared Skye type, blue in colour. Old Kitty was stolen from Manchester and later became the property of J. Kershaw of Halifax. Mr Swift was also a Haligonian but went to Manchester, where he purchased Old Crab. That is the only line we can trace which takes us back as far as 1850, but fifty out of eighty Broken-haired Scotch and Yorkshire Terriers in the stud book have no pedigree.

The famous Huddersfield Ben and his descendants are traced to Old Crab and Old Kitty, but it is plainly evident that there were other fanciers at work in the creation of this wonderful little dog. No person knew more about the origin and growth of the Yorkshire Terrier than the late Mrs M. A. Foster of Bradford, and it was her Huddersfield Ben that perfected the breed. In 1885 Mrs Foster said, regarding the pedigree of the dog Bradford Hero, that all the best dogs for the past thirty-five years were included in him and they were all originally bred from Scotch Terriers and shown as such until a few years back.

Dalziel was of the opinion that the Yorkshire Terrier was 'a conglomeration of the Skye, Paisley or Clydesdale, and the Black-and-Tan Terrier'. It will be noted that all the various breeds of dog mentioned seem to have contributed to the early development of the Yorkshire Terrier, all probably descending from the same original source, and though there is much difference of opinion as to his exact origin, still the same characteristics and terrier instincts have prevailed over the years.

The introduction of the Yorkshire Terrier to the United States of America took place in about 1880, and some American writers of that period, such as Mason, made rather caustic comments on the fact that its type was not very well fixed. It is not difficult to imagine their perplexity as to just what kind of dog was to be the style, show records, for example, indicate that weights varied from 2¾ to 13 lb.

Standard of Points

There are ten clubs serving the interests of the Yorkshire Terrier in Great Britain.

The parent club is The Yorkshire Terrier Club, founded in 1898. Its purpose and those of its fellow societies is to promote through its members the breeding dogs of high standard points. A publication of description, type, and standard of points is available for all breeders, judges, dog-show committees, etc., for guidance and to protect and advance the interests of the breed. This is done by the awarding of cups, trophies, and special prizes, supporting of certain shows, and taking any steps that may be decreed advisable to raise such standards.

The various standard points have a percentage of values as follows:

Formation and terrier appearance	15
Colour of hair on the body	15
Richness of tan on head and legs	15
Quality of texture of coat	10
Quantity and length of coat	10
Head	10
Mouth	5
Legs and feet	5
Ear	5
Eyes	5
Tail (carriage of)	5
Total	100

These were the original points and they were again approved at the Annual General Meeting of the Yorkshire Terrier Club on 16 October 1946, and have not been revised since.

The following revised Standard of the Breed was issued by the Kennel Club in 1986 after general agreement between the Breed Club, the Breed Council and the Kennel Club. It is reproduced with permission of the Kennel Club. The previous standard had been in force since its adoption in 1950.

General Appearance   Long coated, coat hanging quite straight and evenly down each side, a parting extending from nose to end of tail. Very compact and neat, carriage very upright conveying an important air. General outline conveying impression of vigorous and well-proportioned body.

   Characteristics   Alert, intelligent toy terrier.

   Temperament   Spirited with even disposition.

   Head and Skull   Rather small and flat, not too prominent or round in skull, nor too long in muzzle, black nose.

   Eyes   Medium, dark, sparkling, with sharp intelligent expression and placed to look directly forward. Not prominent. Edge of eyelids dark.

   Ears   Small, V-shaped, carried erect, not too far apart, covered with short hair, colour very deep, rich tan.

   Mouth   Perfect, regular and complete scissor bite, i.e. the upper teeth closely overlapping the lower teeth and set square to the jaws. Teeth well placed with even jaws.

   Neck   Good reach.

   Forequarters   Well laid shoulders, legs straight, well covered with hair of rich golden tan a few shades lighter at ends than at roots, not extending higher on forelegs than elbow.

   Body   Compact with moderate spring of rib, good loin. Level back.

   Hindquarters   Legs quite straight when viewed from behind, moderate turn of stifle. Well covered with hair of rich golden tan a few shades lighter at ends that at roots, not extending higher on hindlegs than stifle.

   Feet   Round, nails black.

   Tail   Customarily docked to medium length with plenty of hair, darker blue in colour than rest of body, especially at end of tail. Carried a little higher than level of back.

   Gait/Movement   Free with drive; straight action front and behind, retaining level topline.

   Coat   Hair on body moderately long, perfectly straight (not wavy), glossy; fine silky texture, not woolly. Fall on head long, rich golden tan, deeper in colour at sides of head, about ear roots and on muzzle where it should be very long. Tan on head not to extend on to neck, nor must any sooty or dark hair intermingle with any tan.

Colour   Dark steel blue (not silver blue), extending from occiput to root of tail, never mingled with fawn, bronze or dark hairs. Hair on chest rich, bright tan. All tan hair darker at the roots than in middle, shading to still lighter at tips.

Size   Weight up to 3.1 kgs (7 lbs).

Faults   Any departure from the foregoing points should be considered a fault and the seriousness with which the fault should be regarded should be in exact proportion to its degree.

NOTE: male animals should have two apparently normal testicles fully descended into the scrotum.

In compiling this standard, the aim was to supply a word-picture of an ideal dog. Anyone who aspires to success either as a breeder, exhibitor, or judge would do well to study this standard and devote serious thought to it.

If considered intelligently, it should conjure up a mental picture of a Yorkshire Terrier of the correct type, but since it becomes increasingly evident that a number of breeders either never refer to the standard, or, if they do, fail to grasp the significance of it, it would seem desirable to examine this description to clarify any doubt.

A note of breed clubs for Yorkshire Terrier enthusiasts will be found in Appendix B.

Starting a Kennel

When starting a kennel it is important to consider the space that you have available. If a room in the house can be allotted for the sole use of the dogs, this is ideal, for on wet days, when the garden or run is impracticable, the dogs can then play and exercise without being in the way. It is also a good place in which to groom the dogs, and to have all the necessary equipment away from your own living quarters. It is easy to arrange the sleeping accommodation of the dogs. Have the kennels raised off the floor and out of draughts, but on no account should they be one on top of the other, for in the event of a door being left unlatched the little inmate could fall or jump from such height and dislocate a limb or something even worse.

If an outdoor kennel has to be used, a small building could easily be erected by anyone accustomed to the use of tools at much less cost than a bought one. It should be erected to a definite plan, situated in a sheltered corner, facing south to get as much sunshine as possible.

The prime essentials in such a building are sufficient space for the owner to stand and turn round in easily, otherwise work in the kennel will be difficult. All draughts must be excluded; this is most important. A large window should give sufficient light, and if electricity can be installed so much the better. The sleeping-pens can be arranged round the room, raised well off the floor. In the winter an oil or electric heater will give a comfortable warmth.

A useful addition is a lean-to on one side of the kennel. The land underneath this will keep dry, and if wired in with a gate at one end will make an ideal exercise ground for wet days.

One of the first things to do before erecting a kennel in the garden is to make sure that the local council will not object.

Another point to consider is whether it is too near to your neighbours and likely to be a cause for complaint.

All dogs with the joy of living are noisy at times and one allows for that, but it is up to the breeder, who is educated in the ways of dogs, to see to it that his dogs do not become nuisances. It is one thing when a dog barks at the door-bell ringing, or at a stranger at the garden gate, but quite another if there is continual pandemonium. If corrected in the proper way your dog will become an alert watch-dog and not a coward who barks at every sound.

When only a few dogs are kept, if properly trained they need not be a nuisance, for although a Yorkshire Terrier is by no means a silent animal, he is not a constant yapper. He is protection against intruders in his own domain and should make neighbours feel more secure.

I have never kennelled my dogs outside and I do not recommend it, but for some it may be necessary, and if the following points are kept in mind it can be most successful.

It is important to have a good, safe exercise ground from which the dogs cannot escape into the next garden, or into fields if the kennel is in the country. This sort of thing can lead to much unpleasantness, and if the next-door garden is not secure the dog may easily get into the street, wander away and end in being lost, to both the dog's and the owner's sorrow.

Always keep the exercise ground as free as possible from dirt, then there will be no cause for complaint. If possible, have a sunny spot, but make sure also that there is plenty of shade.

Having the main essential, the kennel, and before buying any stock, it is most important that you should acquire the most comprehensive knowledge of the breed. It has been said that the best way to learn about a breed is to buy a dog of that breed, and take it to a show. This is good common sense: certainly one can quickly learn the good points and the imperfections of the particular dog, and also by careful observation learn many useful tips.

You may find that the dog is really good enough to be the founder of your kennel, but if this is not so do not become too attached to the dog or you will not be able to part with him, and you will find yourself in the position of having a passenger from the start. It is easy enough to saddle oneself with passengers without buying them, so the utmost care should be taken in the selection of stock if you propose to start in this way.

Another method is to buy stock with the idea of breeding. Many people do this without first going into the full ancestry, and then they are disappointed with the results. If you happen to have a natural eye for a dog this is all in your favour and you will quickly learn, but do not be tempted to spend money on any stock before you know what you actually want. Do not imagine yourself even fairly knowledgeable while you are still at the novice stage. Even when you have been in the game for many years you will find there is still a lot to learn. In fact, one never stops learning.

Assuming you have no previous experience at all, what is the best way to start? The first thing to do is to study the standard, and I mean study. Try to visualize the points (as recognized by the Club) on the living animal. Read as much as possible on the subject. Buy one or both of the weekly dog journals: *Our Dogs* or *Dog World*. Read the reports of the judges of the breed at the various shows. Read also the breed news, the articles on general topics, and the advertisements for forthcoming shows. The latter will tell you where and when the shows will be held and if Yorkshire Terriers are scheduled. Make a special point of going to as many shows as possible. The Championship or Open Shows are really the best, although some very good specimens can be seen at the smaller shows, such as Members' or Sanction Shows in which youngsters are schooled into the ways of the ring, and the atmosphere of shows so as to gain confidence for larger shows. Study well all the dogs being shown and try to pick out the winners; it is fun, and you can learn a great deal.

Go along to the benches after judging has finished and have a chat with some of the exhibitors and if you show that you are interested in the breed and keen to learn, most of them will be glad to help. To start off with, do not ask questions that are too pointed, for if you hint that you are on the lookout for really good foundation stock you may find some exhibitors too pressing. Others, however, you will find only too willing to help.

Do not make any decisions hastily; you will need a much wider look round first, and early impressions are not always the best.

While at the ring you may hear comments and even discussions on the virtues or the faults of some of the exhibits, or criticisms of the judge, but remember, when you hear such criticisms, that the judge is the one handling the exhibit, and faults and virtues he sees cannot always be seen by the ringsider. You will be wise to ignore such remarks; there is always somebody who can do a job better than anybody else, but if that someone had the same job he would probably do exactly the same thing. Try to form your own opinion.

Do not miss the opportunity of visiting a good kennel. All sorts of tips can be picked up and a study of the general management would be well worth your while, apart from being interesting.

Try to study pedigrees and strains and begin to form in your own mind the type you propose to use as foundation stock. If you buy a good bitch or two out of a winning strain, not necessarily Champion strain, in my opinion there is no better way of starting. A good age is between seven and twelve months; at that age you can see how well the bitch is developed, and if she will be large enough to be successfully bred from. Never start off with a tiny bitch no matter how well bred and beautiful she may be. Sometimes one is fortunate enough to be able to buy an older bitch who is proved, one having had one litter for preference, and offered for sale only to make room for younger stock. You may be fortunate enough to see some of her litter and can judge their points You should be able to breed from her until a fair age and she will prove her worth.

Take care to examine her thoroughly before buying and see that no small lumps have formed about the milk glands. These are caused by a secretion of milk which has not drained off after her litter were weaned. They may need treatment, for if neglected an abscess may form. Ask lots and lots of questions regarding her actions when she had her litter. Maybe she is not a really good mother, and her puppies had to be hand-fed long before the usual age of weaning, four to five weeks. Maybe she is a hard and difficult whelper. All such questions asked will be a guide to what to expect when she has a litter for you. Sometimes with a first litter the bitch will be a little troublesome, and allowances must be made for this. With subsequent litters she may become a perfect mother.

With the brood bitch puppies, you can watch their growth and enjoy the fun of their puppyhood. You must make sure that they haven't any apparent faults such as an overshot jaw, or ears so placed that they will never be erect. On the other hand, your brood bitches do not have to be the most outstanding puppies to produce good offspring. If you have gone to the trouble of finding out their background, they will most likely produce something very good and will not be so expensive to buy as a beautiful puppy. Like the human race, plain parents often have very beautiful children.

Never on any account buy a bitch, whether puppy or adult, which is nervous or a bad 'doer'. A dog that will not come when called, that will not eat when given good meals, is not worth bothering about and will not make a good brood. Temperament is of great importance. Anything in the way of shyness, nervousness or lack of appetite should be avoided. A brood bitch should have none of these failings, for she will pass them on to her progeny.

Sometimes, of course, these faults can be cured. It may be that a puppy has not been taken notice of, handled sufficiently or even loved. Affection, to a puppy especially, is a great winner of confidence, and you may be able to make something of such a puppy when you know a little more about the breed, but at first it is best to play safe and leave the experimenting until later.

Buying a Puppy

It is a good plan when buying a puppy to take an experienced breeder with you, especially if the breed is not well known to you. To select a puppy from a litter at eight weeks old is something of a problem. Some breeders say they can pick out a future champion at birth. I know from experience, for example, that one can definitely foretell that the colour of a young puppy is going to be good later on, but changes take place so quickly that sometimes the smallest and best-looking youngster may become the largest when mature, and other faults may also become apparent.

First glance at a litter will tell you whether the puppies are healthy. Their coats should shine, and the tiny bit of tan that does show on the feet and over the eyes should be a good colour. One should be able, at so young an age, to pick the puppy up by the loose skin on the back; a tight skin usually denotes an unhealthy state, and that the puppy is suffering either from worms or indigestion. When the puppies are brought out for your inspection, just ignore them. If you do, they will then decide you are not worth making a fuss of and

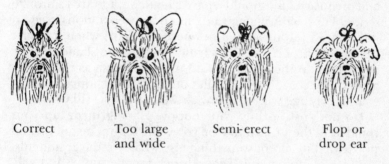

Correct   Too large   Semi-erect   Flop or
                 and wide   drop ear

Ear Carriage

will start to play naturally. You will then be able to observe them and pick out the puppy that takes your eye.

If a male puppy he should have a compact, substantial body, be low to the ground, but not too short of leg. He should be a sprightly mover and have a bright eye. The ears are some-times erect at this age— some are born with erect ears and never put them down— but more often than not they are down during the teething stage; you can easily see by the placement of the ears if they will eventually be erect. They should be well on top of the head, the leather firm to the touch. A floppy ear, set low, with very little or no substance of leather, seldom goes up even with help.

If you are buying a puppy in the hope of making her a brood, see that her back is of a good length. A bitch with a long back can carry puppies more easily than a short, cobby bitch.

No matter the sex of the puppy, examine the mouth. If the jaws are even, all is well. The teeth are barely through at the age of eight weeks so are no guide in choosing. The action is very important; weaving of the front legs, caused by one foot being placed across the other when walking, is a bad fault and is not likely to improve with age. The hind legs should be straight. If there is a tendency for the heels to be turned in, or for the legs to splay from each other, both are equally bad faults.

I have mentioned that there will be slight tan showing over the eyes and on the feet. The body coat at this age will be black and on no account should it have a tendency towards a bronze shade. This colouring may be caused by preparations used on the skin—a puppy sometimes develops scurf when it is first weaned—but, on the other hand, the bronze shade may be something in the breeding and may get worse as the puppy grows. The coat should be silky and soft to the touch; a harsh coat at this age will not grow so well as a soft, silky one.

Do not rush to buy your puppy. Having made up your mind as to the strain and type you want, do not be put off and persuaded to accept something else whatever the arguments. You are planning your kennel stock for the future and will, therefore, be breeding for the improvement of the breed. Whatever age puppy is decided on, it is wise to choose a really good one, rather than spend money on two or three indifferent specimens, however impressive their pedigrees may be.

Occasionally a bitch may be acquired on breeding terms. This means an arrangement between the owner of the bitch and the person to whom she is loaned. Take care to make as many enquiries as possible regarding former experiences during pregnancy and whelping, for you do not want to be saddled with an unsound bitch. Usually the owner of the bitch selects the sire to whom she wants the bitch mated and pays the fees; or maybe she has a stud of her own that she prefers. The first choice of the litter generally goes to the owner, sometimes the third as well; the remainder of the litter becomes the property of the person to whom she is loaned. She is usually defined as the breeder, which in fact she should be, having had all the trouble of the actual whelping and rearing of the puppies, and it is in her name as breeder that the puppies are registered. Two or more litters can be arranged in a similar way, the bitch then becoming the property of the person to whom she was loaned.

This is considered an inexpensive way of starting, but it has its drawbacks since the person to whom the bitch was loaned, after having had all the trials and work of the whelping of the bitch comes off with the second best of the litter.

Breeding terms agreements differ a great deal and may mean anything between two parties. Should any idea of this sort be entertained, do have every detail of the agreement in writing and signed by both parties and registered at the Kennel Club, 1–4 Clarges Street, Piccadilly, London, W1Y 8AB. Really good friends have been known to fall out, so it is very much better to have every detail in black and white, signed and sealed.

A true breeder aims high and will try to breed the best possible dogs; those that are healthy, intelligent, good tempered and a credit to their owners. Try to arrange each mating with the expectation that the progeny will not only be an improvement on the parents but that future generations will maintain the standard. Until an animal is bred from, one cannot be certain which of its inherited qualities it may transmit to its progeny. In establishing a kennel, the greatest stress should be placed on the selection of the bitches, for the strength of the kennel lies in its bitches. The better the average of good bitches in a kennel the better the average of good puppies bred.

This building up of a kennel must, by its nature, be a slow process, but it pays in the long run. There will be setbacks, of course, but do not get discouraged. It has often been said by breeders who have had a run of bad luck, 'No, I'm not going to start again,' but if the urge is in the blood no breeder can resist the temptation to try again.

4

General Management

First, and most important, every dog rightly deserves to be kept healthy, clean and happy. The Yorkshire Terrier is a naturally happy and very healthy dog, being one of the hardiest of the toy breeds. Good management is the result of a real love for a dog, plus a slight knowledge of hygiene and the ability to look ahead and give attention to all details.

Sometimes a fond owner's ignorance, carelessness, or neglect of the basic principles of management, are responsible for disorders that need never have arisen.

A contented dog is not possible without correct management be he the come-hiking pet or the show-ring dandy.

One should aim to assist nature as much as possible by regular feeding, necessary exercise, sleep and correct grooming which together add up to good health; the need for patent remedies will not then arise.

Whether one Yorkshire Terrier is kept, or more than one, there are certain principles of management to be observed in order to get the greatest enjoyment or profit (if you are breeding), or both. There is no point in having pure-bred stock if you are not prepared to spend the necessary time, patience, and money to keep them in the best possible condition.

Routine is appreciate by any dog, especially dinner at the appointed time. If he is not allowed out for exercise at a certain hour he will become restless, and if he is a well-trained dog he will wait until such time as he is let out to relieve himself. This irregular practice, if pursued, may eventually cause weakness of the bladder or damage to the kidneys.

Many Yorkshires are shut up for hours at a stretch and forced to lead a monotonous life in the same place, seeing the same dogs and the same people. The finest thing to keep him the alert little dog he should be is to give him variety and freedom.

Feeding

It is universally admitted that animal flesh is absolutely essential for the dog, and it must be generally accepted that a varied and mixed diet is best suited to him. In estimating the daily quantity of meat, an allowance must be made for the season of the year, because the digestive system and other functions of the body vary under the influence of cold and heat, the cold being stimulating and the heat depressing. If the same quantity of meat is given all the year round, diarrhoea and other disturbances are likely to occur. Yorkshire Terriers cannot take too much meat because they are peculiarly susceptible to its stimulating effect and are quickly disturbed by an excess, the results being an impairment of the blood and an overheated condition of the system, which causes irritation of the skin and, often, falling of the hair.

He is so constituted physically that he can digest both animal and vegetable foods and from them, when given in correct proportions, he will obtain all the nourishment required for the growth of his body and its maintenance.

Onions, garlic, and watercress are credited with medicinal virtues of a marked character, and the first-named two are believed by many to be a sure preventive against, as well as a destroyer of, worms. They are all stimulants and cause increased secretion of saliva and gastric juices and in this way favour the digestion, provided they are used moderately. All vegetables, with the exception of potatoes, are an advantage in the feeding. They not only vary the diet, but render certain other foods more nutritious and wholesome, stimulating the secretion of the digestive solvents and improving the action of the bowels, thus maintaining the purity of the blood.

The farinaceous or starchy foods such as that contained in brown bread, wheat, corn, rice, pearl barley, and the like, are also good additions to a dog's food. Rice is one of the best starchy foods, although poor in tissue-building and energy-producing qualities. It is very nearly pure starch, but must not be despised for this reason, and if it is mixed with meat juices or milk is really a good staple food. It must be cooked well, because starch is composed of solid granules which are not digestible until they have been softened. It is maintained by some that feeding with rice is fat producing, that it is not suitable for Yorkshires, and that if it is given at all it should be only in small quantities. But ideas and results of practice are sometimes at variance. The staple food of most of the toy breeds is rice, the main reason for including it in their diet being that it is cooling and very good for the skin and, therefore, good for the coat. For this reason alone it should be included as being especially suitable.

There are many veterinary surgeons and physicians who believe that the food has a decided influence on the growth of the hair and that starches play the most active part. Probably this theory is correct and certainly experience would seem to substantiate it, for the Yorkshire Terrier is admitted to be the best hair grower among the toy dogs, and in fact of all long-coated breeds. Rice, therefore, is a food that can be relied upon by all.

No fixed rules can be laid down regarding the amount of each ingredient of the mixed diet. The general condition, whether puppy, youngster or adult, must be taken into account and the amount varied accordingly, but a generous quantity of meat should always be given to the adult and the in-puppy bitch.

The main meal should consist of chopped meat (about two-thirds of the entire meal), some crushed cubes, which I will tell you how to make later in this chapter, cooked rice, or a biscuit meal, the latter scalded with the stock from the stewed meat or bone broth. When using stock always bring it to the boil before pouring it on the biscuit, etc.; this will kill any germs, should there be any. A little chopped green vegetable and carrot, a few drops of cod-liver oil or halibut oil, makes an excellent and nourishing meal. Most dogs prefer their food warm, especially in winter, as it seems to make the meal more appetizing. Never give it cold food, no matter what the time of the year is; also, never make the consistency of it too wet; keep it rather like breadcrumbs.

Before myxomatosis destroyed it the English rabbit was one of the cheapest and most nourishing of foods for dogs, and it is hoped it will again be possible to include it in their diet, as it is very good for young or old. It must, however, be cooked correctly. It should be stewed until the flesh falls away from the bone, and here I must stress the absolute necessity for removing all the bone because a tiny fragment can do untold harm. A sheep's head cooked until it is tender, with an onion, carrot, and pearl barley, makes a wonderfully balanced meal and is loved by all dogs. Salt may be added while it is cooking and rice may be used in the place of the pearl barley. This is another instance where care has to be taken to see that all the bones have been removed before it is given to the dog.

Mutton and beef are the main meats included in the diet, but tongue, heart, kidney and liver make a good change. Do not, however, give too much liver, because it tends to cause looseness of the bowels. The process of cooking can be changed to make the meal more appetizing, a roast being something of a treat. All cooked food should be cooked thoroughly; if it isn't, it acts as an irritant and causes digestive upsets and other disturbances. The pressure cooker is most useful and economical for cooking heart and tongue, but do not use it for mutton and beef because it is inclined to impregnate the meat with fat, making it too rich and sometimes causing an upset tummy or sickness.

Give any kind of fish in the place of meat. The herring is especially beneficial as it is rich in oil and provides mineral salts and iodine. Cooked very slowly in its own fat, it is very tasty, but remember, remove all the bones.

Rice pudding, in fact any milk pudding, is a luxury enjoyed by puppies and adults alike. An egg custard, which is so easily digested and for that reason given to invalids, is loved by all dogs. A raw egg given in warm milk, sweetened with honey or glucodin, is very good for a bad-doer, for young puppies, the stud dog or the bitch in whelp. A bitch of mine having had her litter, followed me down the garden to the chicken-house and proceeded to help herself to a warm new-laid egg. Here Nature acted as her guide as to what she really needed. Hardboiled egg is very good for a dog that has had looseness of the bowels, because it helps to bind.

There is much value in finely chopped *raw* cabbage, carrot, watercress and parsley, any or all of which can be added to the meat meal. It is an agreed fact that there is not much value in *cooked* green vegetables, but in my opinion this does not apply to spinach, which is so rich in iron. The iron content in fresh green vegetables helps to correct pale pigmentation. All kinds of fruit, especially apple and orange, seem to be enjoyed, but not by all dogs.

Cheese being very rich in calcium is beneficial especially to the bitch in whelp; it can be grated and sprinkled over the meal.

Variety is a splendid aid to health, but the combination of the various foods is a question of convenience. The all-important factor is quality not quantity.

Feeding an adult dog is quite easy. Never give him too much at any time, for all dogs are greedy and ever ready for titbits, even after a good meal. It is a good idea to make the evening meal his main meal of the day; about six o'clock is a good time. He will then have had a chance for it to digest before he goes to bed and will not be hungry and so will sleep through the night. A few dog biscuits or cubes can be given at midday, or a light meal if he requires it, but many dogs keep quite healthy on the one main meal a day.

The quantity to give a dog varies with the individual. Watch the dog carefully and note his general condition. Measure the amount of food given him during a week, and then strike an average, thereafter giving him the estimated amount as long as he is doing well, and decreasing or increasing it as he puts on or loses flesh. If this plan is wisely followed, there will be no opportunity for him to overfeed. He will lick his plate clean and very likely wish he had a little more, but once in condition he will keep that way. If at the evening meal after a good start he begins to pick over the food for the daintiest morsels, or starts to try to cover up what is left, you will know that he has had too large a portion, and a smaller amount should be given next day.

To ensure that every dog has his full share of food, give each a separate dish. It is best to put each dog in his own compartment to have his meal so that if one dog is off his food the fact can be quickly noted and necessary measures taken. With communal feeding one dog may get too much, while another may have to go short, or one will get the meat and the other what remains.

Always remove the dish after a reasonable time even if the dog has not finished the meal for, if it is left and the dog can pick at it at any old time it soon forms a bad habit, and may make the dog finicky; also the stale food can become contaminated by flies. Never leave food in the hope that a dog will finish it later. Take it right away and at the next feed offer it again. If he still leaves it, examine him to try to find out if he is off-colour or just dainty. Dogs have some second sense of smell, it seems, for often a very good dinner is left only because he has smelt something cooking that is more to his liking. He will throw up his head and sniff in the direction from which the scent is coming.

Most Yorkshires enjoy a drink of milk, sweetened or unsweetened. Milky tea, sweetened with sugar or glucodin, is a special treat. Before retiring, in winter, a warm drink of Ovaltine, malted milk or the like is thoroughly appreciated as a nightcap, and the little ones go to bed satisfied and happy. In the summer a similar drink is enjoyed cold.

A large, tasty shin-of-beef bone, that has been sawn into pieces of convenient size and all the splinters removed, is a great joy, the process of gnawing helping to keep the teeth in good condition, as well as cleaning them. It will last a long time— it should be scrubbed to sweeten it— and besides being a good toothbrush it is a wonderful toy, being tossed about, hidden and found. Oh, the joy a dog can get from a bone!

Care must be taken with any other inmates of the kennel when fresh bones are given out, for the jealous possessor of one will try to take another from his mate, which sometimes leads to a quarrel. It is best to shut the dogs in their respective beds to enjoy their bones in seclusion. It is astonishing that an old bone does not raise the same militancy. An old one will be played with in the garden by all the dogs and jealousy does not seem to exist among them, although sometimes one dog in a kennel may be very possessive about his treasures and not allow any other inmate to share them. One of my little dogs, although now an adult, will not let any of the other dogs have the small woolly toy that he played with when a puppy; it is his very own and how dare one of the others touch it!

The little show dog cannot, of course, have a bone to chew and enjoy, owing to the fact that he would chew off his moustache, which is one of his special features. Oh, the pity of it, for in consequence he tends to lose his teeth at a very early age, but that is one of the penalties of being a show dog. Do not give small soft bones because pieces can chip off and cause great harm, and never give poultry or rabbit bones.

There is an old saying: 'One man's meat is another man's poison'! Nearly everyone can safely eat strawberries, but a few, on eating them, develop a most annoying rash. Nature's first food for every child is milk, and yet there are quite a lot of people who become ill on drinking it. The egg is certainly one of the most harmless of foods, yet instances of illness caused by eating eggs are quite frequent. Not all people are fond of and can digest with equal ease the same kinds of food. So it is with the dog. It is necessary to watch closely to see how a certain diet acts. No two members of the same breed are so constituted that the food suitable for one is precisely as suitable for another. It is a well-known fact that some breeders feed their dogs very largely, and some entirely, on meat, and their dogs do well. Not unnaturally, therefore, they believe it to be the all-important food. On the other hand, there are some who rely wholly on vegetables and starch, and they in turn are as strongly convinced that their diet is the only one. A novice sometimes will accept the theory of the first breeder referred to and feed his dog on flesh, without meeting with the success for which he had hoped. Another follows the other's method and is equally disappointed. From these unfortunate experiments it might seem that both ideas are absolutely wrong, but this is not so. Had either diet been supplemented with other vitamin-giving items, a good, balanced and health-giving meal would have resulted.

Vitamins

Vitamin A increases the resistance to disease. It promotes healthy growth in puppies and is found in animal fat, cod-liver oil, halibut oil, butter, milk and eggs.

Vitamin B. This prevents constipation and improves the nervous system. It is contained in wholemeal bread, yeast and fresh raw vegetables.

Vitamin C is a purifier of the blood and is contained in fresh fruit and in fresh green vegetables.

Vitamin D is necessary to promote bone growth. It is contained in cod-liver oil, halibut oil and liver.

Vitamin E is necessary to promote fertility. A high percentage is contained in wheat germ and oats, and a smaller percentage in eggs, meat and fresh green vegetables.

I mentioned earlier in this chapter that I would describe the way to make cubes. On Sunday, when the family roast is well on the way, cut some wholemeal or wheatmeal bread into cubes, place them in the oven and allow them to become a crisp, golden brown. Store them in an airtight tin where they will keep crisp for quite a time. They are very useful for the morning snack, in the place of dog biscuit, and will not only amuse your dog, but also serve the purpose of helping to clean his teeth.

Sometimes a dog will get food fixed to the roof of his mouth, causing him to choke. This can be very alarming, especially to a novice, for the dog will claw frantically at the sides of the jaw and appear to stand on his head in an attempt to release the obstruction. Do not panic, but gently hold the dog and with your fingers remove the substance or push it to the larger part of the mouth, when it will be swallowed.

Water

Nearly three-fourths of a dog's body consists of water; it constantly parts with a large amount of it through the lungs, the skin and other avenues. In order that health may be maintained, there must in consequence be a constant renewal of this simple yet highly important fluid. Drinking-water, if left near decayed substances, will soon absorb the exhalations and become to some degree poisonous. Also, when so exposed it will take up germs from the surrounding air. It is a well-known fact that if a pail of water is stood in a room that has been freshly painted the smell of the paint is absorbed into the water.

The drinking-water, therefore, should always be above suspicion and the container left scrupulously clean. Instead of any old thing, buy one of the plastic type bowls, which won't break and are very easy to keep clean.

Some who have written on the management of dogs have questioned the advisability of keeping water constantly before the dog, giving as a reason that too frequent lapping may become a habit prejudicial to health. This theory is not a sound one, for the desire for water is increased by frequent indulgences, and they in turn increase tissue-waste change and so multiply the products of tissue waste which result from it. Water removes these waste products as fast as they are formed and in consequence of the various changes the appetite is increased. Water may therefore be said to act as a true tonic. A dog who is closely confined not only drinks more, but actually needs more than one that has his liberty. A dog who exercises freely eliminates the waste products to a certain extent, but a dog who is denied exercise has to depend largely upon water for their removal therefore he drinks more.

Some breeders fail to appreciate the fact that water is indispensable to the welfare of young puppies, and think that sloppy foods, milk, broths, etc., are enough to satisfy their thirst, and furnish them with all the water required to meet the needs of their systems. For these reasons such breeders seldom put down a supply of water for their puppies until they are over seven weeks old. This is a mistaken idea, because puppies are always hungry and if allowed to drink water at an early age take it freely and often, thus lessening their capacity and their desire for food and greatly improving their digestion.

If the digestive fluids of young puppies are less active than usual, indigestion is the consequence. Pure fresh water has a decidedly corrective influence on these fluids and fortifies them, so water can fairly be called a remedy. Puppies should be taught to drink water at the earliest possible age and should always be able to get to a bowl of pure, fresh water. The constant washing of the inner body modifies the appetite, helps to render the digestive fluids more active, allays irritation of the stomach and washes the food remnants out of the stomach. All this must add greatly to the dog's health.

Exercise

This is an A to Z glance at the physiology of exercise. A very large part of the body consists of muscular tissue, which contains nearly one-quarter of the whole of the blood supply. By means of this muscle tissue, fully one-fourth of the nerve energy stored up in the body is turned into work. Every muscle has blood-vessels and nerves, and fresh blood is supplied to it by the heart, through the arteries and a fine network of small blood-vessels. The vessels open into and are continuous in the veins and they in turn are united into larger vessels that finally connect with the channel by which the blood is returned to the heart.

As soon as a muscle begins to work the bloodstream passes through changes in quality. The blood which enters is bright red in colour, is rich in oxygen, but poor in carbonic acid, while that which leaves it is a dark blue in colour and a higher temperature, because it has lost much of the oxygen and has taken up a large amount of carbon dioxide and various other products resulting from chemical changes having taken place.

The muscle receiving a full supply of fresh blood can freely and rapidly discharge its waste matter and by proper food in sufficient quantities and an abundance of pure fresh air renders the blood rich in nutritious elements and oxygen, thus increasing health. The muscles are not the only part of the body to benefit by exercise for it increases the rapidity of the flow of blood into the heart, which vital organ also works more vigorously, causing a larger amount of blood to be sent through the lungs which, in turn, quicken the speed of breathing and so more oxygen is absorbed. In consequence, the skin and other organs of secretion and excretion are brought into action.

By depriving a dog of exercise the digestive organs are among the first to show signs of distress, their work becoming sluggish, and performance imperfect, with the result that the food constituents taken up from them by the blood are not properly oxidized. Drainage of the bad products is, in consequence, impeded not only in the muscles but also in all the organs which constitute the waste disposal system. The waste that accumulates through its poisonous action lowers vitality, weakens digestive organs, sometimes causing serious disorder, muscles become soft and flabby, and general ill-health follows.

The amount of exercise required by Yorkshire Terriers varies and it would be quite impossible to fix a rule applicable to all. Although it is usual when dogs are let out into their playground for them to leap and scamper about, they sometimes, like children, need encouragment, and to obtain the greatest benefit from exercise it must be made attractive and enjoyable. It is a good plan to teach a young dog to run after a ball and retrieve it, so that if he must be denied his usual stroll with his master or mistress, he can by this means limber up very quickly and at the same time gain enjoyment. Never let him get too fatigued, however, for this will undo all the good derived from the game.

The show Yorkshire needs exercise as well as his more fortunate brothers. Although he cannot be taken on long walks, he can and should have as much freedom as possible, including a romp in the garden, but not when the younger members of the kennel are out for exercise, because if his long hair is tied up, the puppies—and older dogs—will think it a wonderful opportunity for having fun, hanging on to his hair and playing tug-of-war, until quite a lot of hair is pulled out. If the time can be spared, be in the garden with him and play ball with him, or anything that will give him as much exercise as possible.

If he has to be exercised in the street, keep him firmly on a lead. I know there is no freedom in this for any dog, but it is dangerous for him to be in the street off a lead. I know several people who own obedient dogs and who indulge in this most foolish practice. If questioned on this subject the answer invariably is: ' Oh, he is so well behaved and so well trained, he would not go any further than a few steps from me.' An unforeseen incident, however, resulting in fright could easily lead to disaster and even prove fatal, not only for the dog, but also to mankind.

The best kind of lead for a Yorkshire is one that is fastened after slipping over the head, or a collar and lead. A bridle tends to break off the body coat around the shoulders, giving the dog a scruffy look.

The pet, especially the larger Yorkshire, enjoys to the full a long walk in the country, a park or any open space. He has such stamina that he can compete with his much larger brothers, and I have known a German Shepherd get tired much more quickly than his Yorkshire companion. (Incidentally, the two dogs were inseparable friends; the Yorkie usually to be found between the front legs of the GSD when resting.)

If you have a good garden to which the dog has free access, or a lawn on which he can play, that will provide enough exercise for a small toy. It is astonishing how well a trained dog behaves in a garden. If checked as a puppy from going on the flower-beds, he will keep off them, and if a ball is accidentally thrown there will hesitate before trespassing to retrieve it. Immediately the command 'Get it' is given, he will straightway go and bring the ball back.

It is most unwise to let any dog run about in garden or field when the sun is very hot. The best time for exercise is first thing in the morning and in the evening, but the dog should be let out particularly after resting.

It must be stressed that dogs should not be exercised on grass only; it is necessary that they should be allowed to run on gravel or similar hard surfaces. A hard road helps to tighten up the feet and keep the pads hard and the nails short.

A word of warning if you are taking your dog for a walk in the country. If you come across grazing cattle, keep him on a firm lead, otherwise he may be tempted to run amongst them, thinking it is fun; the result could be a summons from the farmer, or even an injured dog. Chickens seem to have a fatal fascination for some dogs, often resulting in the dazed hen having a bare patch and the dog a mouthful of feathers.

Grooming

For this very necessary operation use a good brush, preferably one of bristle, but not too hard, the kind that was popular with women years ago before nylon was invented. Nylon bristles should be avoided because they break the hair. A steel comb will be needed, one with the teeth well spaced at one end and close together at the other; a Number 80 made by Spratts Patent Ltd is very good. Have also a small bowl of water in which to moisten the brush from time to time. This eliminates the risk of breaking off the ends of the hair which are so intensely fine that they break very easily.

If the coat is very tangled, wet the part thoroughly and gently separate the hairs before attempting to brush. Do the underneath first, so that when the longer hair on the back is to be done the dog need not be turned upside down. Start by turning the dog on his back, on your lap; he will not object to this if he has been submitted to the treatment from an early age. Moisten the brush and brush all the underneath coat and the legs. Do not make the coat too wet or the process of grooming will take longer than necessary.

Deal with the coat underneath thoroughly then turn the dog over and first brush the body coat up the wrong way. This stimulates the blood into the roots and makes the dog feel good. Next, brush the coat into the usual position, always keeping a centre parting. Last of all, brush the head and face, covering the eyes with your thumb, and brushing the top-knot, or fall, away from the nose. The sides of the head and the moustache are brushed in the same manner. Always protect the eyes, for the slightest dab from the brush may cause much discomfort, and sometimes damage to the eye. After brushing thoroughly you will find the comb slips through the hair easily, using the wide end first and then the close end. Never use the comb too much.

If the top-knot is long enough, it can be tied with a piece of ribbon, or put in a cracker of tissue paper, to keep it out of the dog's eyes, also his dinner. It can get very sticky if left free. All these operations can be comfortably carried out with the dog on your lap, but if you prefer, have the dog standing on a table for all grooming except the underneath. A quick brush and comb-through each day, with a thorough grooming once a week will keep the coat in good condition. A Yorkie is never tidy-looking. He is lovely one minute but after a very short time his appearance changes completely. Do not worry about this as long as you know that he has been well groomed.

While going over the dog thoroughly, close inspection can

easily be made to see if he has picked up any fleas. This may easily happen in the hot weather, for birds and hedgehogs leave them in the garden, and it can be quite alarming to an owner who never dreamt that such a thing could happen to *his* dog.

If a Yorkie is exercised in a field where sheep have been grazing, he is liable to pick up lice or ticks which may cause considerable distress. They are difficult to see at first and by fastening themselves to the dog's skin cannot be removed easily. Wash with an insecticidal shampoo; there are several very good ones on the market. They usually clean the dog, but a further wash may be necessary.

Dust the bedding with an insecticide once a week; in addition to grooming, carefully examine the eyes, ears, teeth, feet, and the anal gland. These items are dealt with at greater length in another chapter, but they are mentioned here so that you will remember to include them in the general routine.

The daily grooming is, in the end, a time-saver. If a Yorkshire Terrier is groomed regularly he will need bathing only occasionally. He is not a type of dog which has a smelly skin and will not therefore have to be washed for this reason, provided, of course, he has not been rolling in any foreign matter, or has been in a very dirty place. If he has, it will be necessary to bath him, and he should be scolded, for bathing is something one does not want to have to do too often.

It is unnecessary to put grease on the coat to promote its growth, for his inner condition will look after this. Prospective dog-owners sometimes seem to be put off buying a Yorkshire, having the idea that it will always have to be drenched in oil. This is not so, although the show dog must have a little oil on his coat because he has to be bathed rather often to attend shows. This dries up the natural oil, which has to be replaced by external application. After a short period, however, the skin will again supply the hair with its natural oil.

Sleeping

Only the very old and the very young require artificial heat in their beds. The main danger to dogs sleeping in too warm an atmosphere is the sudden change of temperature when let out of doors. A little woolly coat is a safeguard against a chill, but it should be taken off as soon as the dog comes back into the house.

Every dog should have a bed of his own to which he can retire in the daytime if he so wishes. It is most important that his bed should be well raised off the floor, for even in a well-constructed house draughts exist, and these can be very dangerous. Find him a cosy corner out of the way of intruders, for if he is very comfortable he should not want to occupy the best armchair. I said 'should not want to', but it is by no means unusual that as soon as someone leaves a warm chair the dog occupies it. The slogan of the Yorkshire Terrier is comfort!

The Yorkshire is a hardy dog and can stand a lot of cold, but it hates a draught. Draughts from overhead are just as bad as those on the floor, consequently the best type of bed is a covered box raised a few inches from the floor, with an opening at one side. The entrance should be large enough to facilitate easy cleaning and if a movable slat is placed along the bottom of this opening the bed will be kept in place. There are many kinds of small kennel, with barred doors, for indoor use, and anybody who has a knowledge of simple carpentry can make these for himself quite cheaply. They are ideal for the owner of several dogs, for in addition to serving as sleeping and resting quarters they facilitate feeding. Each dog soon gets to know his own pen and at feeding-time will jump into his own compartment in eager anticipation of his meal, and will show a distinct preference for this type of sleeping accommodation. Although shut in alone at night he loves the cosiness of his bed and should there be any disturbance during the night the owner knows for certain which dog is needing attention.

Newspaper helps to keep a bed warm in winter and cool in summer. It should be placed in the bottom of the box and a warm woolly supplied for extra warmth in the winter. A Yorkshire loves to snuggle down in the depths of a woolly, although some prefer a mattress, the cover of which should be made of a washable fabric. It is essential that the dog be kept warm; he will sleep more contentedly. Be very careful that he is not given damp bedding: this could cause a chill and even rheumatism.

The bedding should be taken out each day and shaken to ensure that any foreign substances, the result of sickness or the like, are removed, for all dogs have the habit of covering up such an accident. Change the rug in the bed at least once a week; it is essential that the dog's bed should be as clean as one's own.

A curtain can be fixed across the opening to be drawn across at night; this not only keeps out the draught but darkens the interior, adding still more comfort. The pen is easily kept clean, especially if the inside is painted. Keep it wiped down with water with a little veterinary disinfectant added, but do not use disinfectant containing carbolic, because if the dog should lick at the woodwork some of the carbolic could get into his stomach and so cause an upset. Any method that results in perfect cleanliness and a sweet-smelling atmosphere is ideal, for nothing is more offensive than a nasty, doggy smell.

5

The Brood Bitch

A bitch usually comes into season for the first time between the age of nine and twelve months, but the age varies with individuals, some starting much earlier and others being well over one year. If a bitch is very young at her first heat or season, it is very unwise to have her mated because she is not yet mature. At ten months or more it is safe if all the other important factors are also right. One should be sure that she is well up to size, not too fat and not too thin. It is not wise to try to breed from a very tiny Yorkie—5½ to 6 lb. is an ideal weight—but some people do breed successfully from the tiny ones, although if there is trouble a caesarian operation has to be perfomed. Sometimes the puppies do not always survive and one loses the mother. it is therefore better to have a slightly larger bitch.

Do not delay breeding from a maiden bitch much later than two years of age. (A maiden bitch is one who has not had a litter.) After this age the whelping will be much more difficult as the body gets more set and the muscles will not do their work properly.

Spring is the most favourable time of the year for whelping, because when the puppies have reached the weaning stage they can be put out of doors for a few hours, at least on fine days, to get the benefit of the sun's rays. They are then sure to gain in health, strength and vitality with much greater rapidity than when kept within four walls. Where pure fresh air and sunshine is denied during early life, the future is greatly prejudiced. Some breeders make a rule to mate their bitches only at this time of the year.

It is a good plan to be prepared for the time when the bitch should come into season. Be sure she is clean inside and out; this means freedom from worms and any irritation to the skin. The first stage of the heat or coming into season starts with the swelling of the vulva, when there will be a slight discharge. The second stage is marked by the discharge becoming blood-coloured, a stage that usually lasts about ten days. Some bitches are extremely careful about their toilet, and by continual licking keep themselves so clean that only close inspection will tell you that she is in season. The third stage, and the time that is best for the mating to be effected, is when the colour has died away, leaving the bitch swollen and a little damp. Around the tenth to the fourteenth day from when the bitch started to show colour is usually best for mating her.

It is almost impossible for a bitch to pass through a season without her condition being discovered, although sometimes, when the discharge is very scanty and a bitch keeps herself very clean, it may be difficult for the novice to discern it, but there is usually a slight change in her demeanour, characterized by her being restless, and an increased show of affection. The attraction she offers to the opposite sex must, of course, give some indication that this period is near; nevertheless it may be rather difficult to fix the best time for this particular type to be mated.

The conclusion to be drawn from this is that although the stages of season vary, and while some bitches will not permit the approach of a dog, or in other words are not ready, before the end of the second week, others have reached this stage by the end of the first week. No rule can be laid down that will meet all cases, and the only safe way is to examine the bitch each day to ascertain what stage she has reached. Some go off heat extremely quickly, while others will still be serviceable at three weeks after the show of colour.

Do book the service of the stud you think will be suitable well in advance, then there will be no disappointment. Tell the dog's owner when you expect your bitch to come into season and the dog will be reserved for near that date.

If you are sending the bitch any distance, and it will mean her staying away for a few days, send her while she is still showing colour. The owner of the stud can then decide the best time and there will be no chance of your having left it too late. If you are taking her for the mating and returning home the same day, allow yourself plenty of time; a mating cannot be hurried, especially if the bitch is a maiden. With a proved bitch it is not so important, but for either, allow her to rest after the journey. Before she is introduced to her mate, a short walk, which will allow her to relieve herself, is a good idea. After the mating, give her another short rest before the journey home.

If the bitch has to be sent by rail for the service, I must stress the necessity of a well-ventilated and safe travelling-box or basket. It should be large enough for her to be able to stand up straight and to move around in comfort. Be quite sure that it has a sensible door with secure fastenings, and it should be rainproof. Put a collar on the bitch, but not the lead, as this may become entangled and cause harm. A clearly addressed label, showing the name, address and telephone number of the person to whom the bitch is being sent, should be tacked securely on the box and another label, stating her pet name and the name and address of her owner, is a good idea in case there should be delay.

Pay the stud fee at the time of the mating. A receipt should be received giving details of the date of the mating, date of whelping and any other arrangements. A second mating is usually given free if no puppies arrive, but there must have been a clear understanding about this at the time of the service, and it should be referred to on the receipt.

When the bitch is home again keep her fairly quiet for a day or two. Some bitches remain attractive to the male, even after they have been mated, so great care must be taken to ensure that no possible accident can occur. A week may elapse before her condition is again normal.

During the first five weeks of pregnancy, the bitch can enjoy her normal routine and her usual diet will be sufficient. Do not fuss over her but at the same time do not let her exercise too much. Boisterous gambolling with her kennel mates or following you up and down stairs, or jumping should all be avoided.

When conditions are normal the period of gestation, or the carrying of young, is sixty-three days. There are exceptions, of course, and a day or two either way is not uncommon and should not be cause for alarm. Puppies born five days early can be quite healthy and strong. One of my bitches always has her litter, quite easily, five days early, and the litter does not suffer in any way.

When it is established that the bitch is going to have puppies— usually this is known after the fifth week— increase her feed. Give an additional meat meal at midday so as not to overload her stomach by an increased amount at her dinner-time. Cod-liver or halibut oil, if not part of the usual diet, is very beneficial all through her pregnancy. Callo-Cal D Oral (Colloidal Calcium with Vitamin D) or any canine preparation containing calcium, should be given because this helps with the bone formation. A bitch will sometimes collapse when her puppies are any age up to six weeks because they have taken all the calcium from her body. Calcium injections then become urgently necessary, so it is much better to give the bitch calcium before the puppies are born. Milk is very good for her and her daily ration should be increased. To this I add the necessary dosage of Callo-Cal D. Clean fresh water should always be available for her.

About two weeks before she is due to whelp, get her accustomed to sleeping in the box in which she is to have her puppies. It is most upsetting to any bitch, especially one whelping for the first time, to be given a new sleeping place at the last moment. Most prefer to have their puppies in a bed they know and are used to. See that it is placed in a nice cosy corner with not too much light. If a bed is not provided in time she will find seclusion in some inaccessible place and any movement, once the whelping has started, may cause complications.

The best type of whelping box is one on legs, divided into two compartments by a movable slat. Each compartment should have a door, one solid, for making the enclosed section cosy and private, the other, of wire, to provide a light run for the puppies when they are old enough, and additional space for the bitch to move around in should she feel cramped. The dividing slat between the two compartments will stop the puppies wandering into the other side and so getting cold. A lid should go over the whole top, hinged so as to be able to take the mother out. This is to avoid the danger of the puppies falling out, as can so easily happen when there is a large litter and the door is of the type that opens outwards. A kennel constructed as described is very easily cleaned.

On the floor of the whelping kennel have a piece of mackintosh and on this place numerous sheets of newspaper which will not only provide warmth but also soak up any moisture, and can easily be disposed of. The warm bedding should not be of a knitted weave. The fine claws of the puppies catch in knitted material and they are inclined to drag it about the kennel. You may wish to purchase one of the dog beds now on the market. Some are very good for puppies to be on; their tiny claws do not get caught up and any wetness will soak through on to paper placed beneath, so keeping the puppies on a dry surface. These beds wash well and last for years. If you buy a large piece, which is cheaper, and cut it into smaller pieces you will always have one clean. Vetbed is one type I have used. It can be purchased from Vetbed (Animal Care) Ltd, Lother Way, Garforth, Leeds or at most of the General Championship Shows.

As the time draws near for the bitch to have her litter,

Whelping kennel

Ch. Luna Star of Yadnum (*Sally Anne Thompson*)

Ch. Pretty Debbie of Yadnum

Huddersfield Ben *c.* 1865

Ted *c.* 1890

Overdale Marquis *c.* 1890

Ch. Harringay Remarkable

Ch. James of Soham

The author with Ch. Midnight
Gold and Emperor of Yadnum
(*Croydon Times*)

Emperor, Midnight Gold and
Timothy of Yadnum

Ch. Elmslade Galahad of Yadnum and Ch. Golden Button of
Yadnum (*Sally Anne Thompson*)

do keep a careful watch on her movements. Daily exercise should be continued right up to the time of whelping, and a quiet walk will often hasten on a slow birth. A good addition to her diet is a Raspberry Leaf preparation. This seems to help with the whelping and the bitch seems to clear up more quickly after the birth of the puppies. Denes make a Raspberry Leaf Tablet; these can be bought from a Health Food Shop or from their stall at most of the general Championship Shows.

Usually on the day before whelping, and in some cases a little earlier, a very noticeable change occurs in the bitch. She is nervous, will occasionally shiver, no matter how warm her bed, is dejected, listless in her movements and has a grieved and rather despondent expression in her eyes. There is a tendency to shrink away when at liberty to do so, or if she is in her bed she will not come out when called. She will make and remake her bed, scratching it up and tumbling it around. If she is on paper she will tear it up into tiny pieces. These are the usual signs of labour being near.

The characteristic of stealing away to a quiet corner has been accepted by some as evidence that the bitch urgently desires solitude and in consequence they think she should be left alone until she has had her puppies. As a matter of fact, it is not an instinctive tendency peculiar to giving birth, but is common to other experiences of a painful nature: for instance, a dog suffering from constipation, which gives him a pain in his tummy, will often hide away until the pain has subsided. The bitch in the wild state sought seclusion so that she might remain hidden and out of harm's way, but the domesticated bitch cannot resist the kindness and sympathy of her mistress or the person looking after her. All dogs love human companionship at these times. If a bitch really prefers to be left alone, just leave her, but few breeders are not sincerely concerned during the whelping period. Usually they are near and watching events.

When the tearing up of the paper begins it is an imminent sign that puppies are on the way. The fact that the bitch has refused food is also another sign. Leave her alone and try to avoid noises. The bitch is quite likely to be making her bed a whole day before labour actually starts, so be on the alert for the first sign of straining. When the labour pains really start she may pant and breathe quickly and may be very restless.

The first puppy may be born in a few minutes after the beginning of the pains, but sometimes an hour or more will elapse. The bitch will rest between the straining to gather strength. If no puppy has been born after three hours, and the pains have been strong, or should the pains cease altogether, send for a veterinary surgeon. It is always wise to book a veterinary surgeon. Let him know well in advance when your bitch is due to whelp just in case you need his advice and skill.

The first thing to be noticed in a normal whelping is the protrusion from the vulva of a membraneous sac in which the puppy is enclosed. With each pain the bulb-like sac will become larger, starting with a tiny bulb only as large as the little fingertip. This sac contains a watery fluid in which the puppy has been protected during gestation. With each pain, or bearing down (usually the bitch uses her back feet to press on the side of the whelping box for extra help), the sac becomes enlarged and after several pains will be expelled entirely from the body. She will now break the sac, so releasing the puppy.

If the pains do not enlarge this sac it will recede into the body as the bitch breathes in. With the next pain make a close examination. You may see the reason for the delay and a tiny foot may protrude. This is because the puppy is being born in the wrong position, feet first. This is termed a breech birth.

Try with a small piece of clean, soft linen to catch hold of the foot between the thumb and finger. Hold on as tightly as possible so that when the bitch takes a breath the puppy does not recede into her body again. With her next pain, very gently pull with an upward tilt, but whatever you do, try your hardest not to let go, for if the puppy goes back into the bitch only a veterinary surgeon's skill can deliver the puppy.

Sometimes a puppy may appear to be stuck half-way out of the vulva. If the bitch has been straining for some time and is unable to expel it, take a piece of linen, grasp the puppy round the body and pull it out. It is most important, however, that the pulling must be applied only when the bitch strains so that the two actions coincide. A puppy thus born has usually come feet first. The head and shoulders, being the largest part, have caused a stoppage when coming through the pelvic arch.

The bag, while sometimes ruptured during labour, is as a rule intact, and when this is so the bitch will at once proceed to open it with her teeth. The ripping of the membrane must be done immediately otherwise the puppy may suffocate. If a bitch's teeth are poor, or for some other reason she is unable to puncture the bag—sometimes the membranes are of unusual thickness—this part of the bitch's duty will have to be performed by the attendant as promptly as possible. The puppy must be freed quickly otherwise it can drown in the fluid contained in the sac, or for the reason I stated earlier, suffocate. Tear the bag open by pinching at the side with the thumb and finger or, if preferred, cut with a pair of sterilized scissors.

Immediately the puppy is released, the bitch will start to clean it, quite vigorously and roughly, and by licking and rolling it from side to side, cause it to cry and breathe. This treatment acts as a stimulant and excites vigorous movement. The bitch will then, somewhat leisurely, bite off the umbilical cord, one end of which is attached to the middle of the puppy's abdomen and the other to what is called the afterbirth, a mass that looks not unlike a clot of dark blood and is usually about the same size as the puppy. Sometimes the afterbirth does not come away with the puppy, so care should be taken to see that it does. Sometimes it will come away after the next puppy, but if it doesn't, get expert advice. If allowed to remain in the bitch it will cause trouble and the complications that ensue may prove disastrous. Breeders differ on whether the bitch should be allowed to consume the afterbirth. In the wild state, by consuming the afterbirth the mother is provided with food which she might not be able to obtain until well enough to go hunting, but the domesticated dog doesn't need to worry about this since her owner will provide all she requires.

The severing of the umbilical cord should be left until the mother is able to attend to the operation herself. It is made up of many tiny blood-vessels that require the kind of treatment that she is best fitted to give. If it is cut with scissors immediately after the puppy's birth it will cause haemorrhage. If the bitch fails in her work, however, and you have to attend to the operation yourself, employ one of the two following methods: first, hold the cord near to the puppy's body, and with the thumb and fingernails shred the cord until broken; alternatively, about five minutes after the puppy's birth, tie the cord with a thread about two inches from the puppy's abdomen, then cut it with a pair of scissors. There should be little likelihood of bleeding from the navel if these instructions are followed carefully.

The average length of time between the arrival of each puppy is half an hour, and during the greater part of this the mother will rest quietly and may even seem to sleep. The period of time may be much shorter, however, the next puppy following almost before the mother has had time to clean the first. On the other hand, a much longer period may elapse, but provided the bitch just rests, do not worry, it merely means she is just having a slow confinement. Whatever type she is, the first routine will be repeated by the second and subsequent puppies until she has had the whole litter. If the firstborn was a breech birth, however, it does not follow that the rest of the litter will be born in the same way. Generally they are born quite naturally.

Some breeders take each puppy away until all the litter has been born, the bitch not seeming to mind. If she gets very agitated, however, and tries to get to her puppies when she hears them whimper, let her have them with her. She will seem to sit on them, or will push them round the bed, but she will not hurt them and it will be better for her if it calms her.

If the bitch gets exhausted and cannot be botherd to clean her puppy and the puppy appears lifeless as the result of a long birth, take it into the hands, which must be very warm, and roll it from one hand to the other. This movement will be like the licking of the mother, and with perseverance you may be rewarded with a squeak denoting that you have saved the puppy's life. Sometimes a little of the fluid may get into a puppy's mouth, and to prevent it going down into the lungs you should hold the puppy upside down, when the fluid will run out. With a clean piece of linen then gently wipe out the mouth. In all probability the puppy will gasp and splutter, but if when it is put to its mother it begins to suckle all should be well.

The natural instinct of a puppy is to suckle within the first two or three hours, but if it doesn't do this, its chances aren't very good. A good way to get a puppy to suckle is to take it in the right hand, with its back on your palm, grasping it well forward so that the thumb and forefinger reach to the little one's mouth, then press inwards at the back of the puppy's jaws, and so force open the mouth. Now with thumb and forefinger of the other hand, hold the nipple of the bitch and insert it into the puppy's mouth. You may have to use a little patience, but persistence will bring success.

The person to whom the bitch is most deeply attached should be the one to look after her; others, although she may know them well, may not be so successful with her. As an example, a strong, healthy bitch of mine, who had had several large litters successfully and never lost a puppy, whelped while I was abroad. My daughter, with whom she was, in the ordinary way, quite happy, looked after her during the confinement. The bitch had three puppies, a small litter for her, one of which, a well-developed puppy, died after a few days through no apparent cause. A veterinary surgeon had to be called to the bitch because she was running a temperature for no apparent reason, and the vet could attribute the trouble only to the fact that the bitch was fretting for me. I had always attended to her when she had had her other litters and apparently no one else would do. This was the first time she had needed a vet in all her seven years.

During the whelping operation the owner of the bitch may occasionally be able to render valuable assistance, but he should never interfere so long as the mother is doing her work well. If it is necessary to help, be gentle, easy in movement and act with firmness and without hesitation.

Let the bitch be in a fairly warm room, free from draughts, noise and visitors. One of the important things in rearing puppies is for them to be warm. Whatever time of the year, it is almost impossible to have the birthplace too warm, so always provide a well-covered hot-water bottle so that the puppies do not come in direct contact with the heat. The warmth is also comforting to the mother. Maintain the extra heat for at least two weeks, or until the eyes open in summer-time, or until the puppies leave their mother in winter-time. Warmth is an essential for contented puppies.

Give the bitch a warm, milky drink when all the puppies have been born; the tired mother will then settle contentedly with her babies, licking and drying them until they are shining and happy. They will keep sucking away, and although no milk will be extracted for some time they will get a watery fluid which acts as a gentle purgative and keeps them happy until the milk comes in.

It is advisable to test each milk gland, by gently squeezing it, to see that the milk has come in and to make sure that all the puppies are sucking properly with the tongue curled around the teat and the tiny front feet pressing against the mother. It is a heart-warming sight to see a contented litter and a very happy mother.

For the first twenty-four hours give small drinks of warm milk sweetened with honey, or Glucodin with a raw egg beaten up and added to it, or infant cereal. Do not give a heavy meal for a day or two. After the second day the bitch can have some wholemeal rusks soaked in good meat broth, or some fish. From then onwards she can resume her usual diet, but the quantity should be increased as she has not only herself but her family to feed. Give an additional meal to her usual diet with lots of milky drinks. Continue with cod-liver oil or halibut liver oil, and the calcium, for she will need plenty of nourishment.

Watch the action of the mother's bowels: the motion will at first be loose after whelping. If it persists too long, give a little well-boiled rice or arrowroot. If she is too costive, give a little paraffin. From the vulva there will be a dark red discharge, in some cases almost black, but do not worry as this is quite usual. As time goes on the colour will lighten and disappear. Some bitches are much more profuse than others and may have the discharge for quite a long time. Bathe her each morning and evening with a little veterinary antiseptic in warm water to keep her comfortable.

Some bitches have to be taken from their puppies to relieve themselves and will immediately want to fly back to their family. Usually, if a fresh hot-water bottle is put in with the puppies, she will realize that they are being looked after, that no harm will come to them, and will go out. If you go with her, she will not be so suspicious; a bitch with a contented mind will not be affected with milk troubles. Never let a stranger see the puppies while the mother is with them; always wait until she is out of the way. Never let a stranger handle them, for the mother will know, her sense of smell being so sensitive. If you do, it may be some time before she is really sure that nothing is amiss and settles down again.

All bitches differ in regard to their need for milk-producing food. A bitch which has had a large litter, and only one or two of which have survived, may have a too generous supply of milk for her remaining puppies. Her milk and liquid feeds should be reduced and she should be given more meat. On the other hand, a bitch whose puppies are not satisfied needs more eggs, milk, honey, and good broth to make up the deficiency. When the teats fail to respond as they ought and their supply remains scanty, the mother must be encouraged to drink freely of all liquids, including water, in order to secure an increase.

Unfortunately it is impossible, even twenty-four hours after whelping, to determine whether the quantity of milk will be large or small, and breeders of experience, far from being certain, are able to form only a probable diagnosis. The outlook may be considered favourable if at the time of whelping the breasts are large and a fairly good flow of milk has been established. The chances are also increased when there has been a previous litter, for in many instances the quantity of milk is notably greater after the second and third litter. When a bitch has not been wisely and generously fed during gestation, a scanty supply of milk will be the rule. When the bitch is in a healthy condition, her milk supply will be enough to feed her litter no matter what the size. Nature working this one out for herself.

The health of the nursing mother is of the greatest importance. If her constitution is poor, then her milk supply can never be abundant; moreover, what little she has will be vitiated and unwholesome, if not absolutely poisonous. Many puppies die off quickly after birth due to this condition.

Puppies denied sufficient milk or having poor milk can easily be detected. The abdomen, instead of being rounded out and a little resistant to pressure, is quite flat, the walls being relaxed and flaccid. They sleep much of the time and seem unwilling to make any attempt to feed, and when taken in the hand are limp and feeble. These symptoms are those of weakness and point to starvation.

At the age of three weeks the puppies will show interest in lapping by licking the mother's dish; then is the time to teach them to lap. Give them, at first, a little warm milk sweetened with honey or Glucodin. Try to feed each puppy separately and give each only as much as it will readily lick off the plate.

At four weeks, a little given twice a day helps the bitch. The best time is when the dam is away from them because they will not be so hungry when she returns, and less eager to tear at her. She will at once get busy washing them and generally cleaning them up, for at the start of feeding themselves, they almost fall into the dish and get food over themselves. Often the mother will vomit her food, the natural instinct for supplying her young with predigested food until such time as they can masticate their own. Therefore, chop up mother's food very finely; you do not want a puppy to choke.

By this time, four weeks old, the puppies will be well up on their feet, and it will be noticed that the dam will leave them a little more each day, seeking the seclusion afforded by the other compartment of the kennel, the dividing slat keeping the puppies in the other compartment. At six weeks the puppies can be weaned from their mother. Her milk will quickly dry up and quite often she will no longer bother about her offsprings.

The bitch will invariably lose her coat during and after whelping, and the puppies scrambling over her and clawing at her does not help. Sometimes the claws of the puppies are so sharp that the mother suffers great discomfort by their scratching at her breasts when they feed. With a sharp pair of scissors or nail-clippers snip off the pointed tips. If she carries a long coat it is advisable to tie this up, especially around the anus, because it will be easier to keep her clean. She should be bathed each day to keep her fresh and free from germs. A little

Dettol in warm water makes a good wash. Always dry her thoroughly, as she will quickly return to her puppies, and a damp mother is not good for them or herself.

If a litter has to be given to a foster-mother the quality of the bitch does not matter, for a mongrel will do as well as a pure bred, and sometimes even better. The question of size is not a very important one, but for preference it would be ideal to have the two bitches about the same size. What is of the utmost importance is that the foster-mother should be in good health, have a kindly disposition and, imperatively necessary, that she be free from skin trouble or vermin.

If it can be arranged, have a foster-mother who has whelped about a day earlier than the bitch whose duties she is going to take on, although milk three or four days older than the adopted family is usually well digested. The transfer of the puppies should be made as soon as signs indicate that their own mother will be unable to feed them. Delay can be fatal.

If the foster-mother is keeping all or some of her own family, a wise course to pursue in making the transfer is to take both litters and put them in the same basket, keeping them together for a few hours without the mother. During this time the foster-mother will fill up with milk, and because this gives her some discomfort she will generally receive the strangers with the same joy as her own. If, however, there is delay in putting the puppies to her, they should be held to her breasts, and she must be made to understand that she has no choice in the matter and that everything is all right. Do be careful and keep a watchful eye on her. If all goes well for the first day, no unnecessary worry need be experienced.

It sometimes happens that a bitch, although she has never been mated, will possess maternal instincts and act in exactly the same way as a bitch about to have a family. This is called a false pregnancy. She will make her bed and if she has any toys with which she plays, she will gather them into her bed and tuck them into her body as if they were puppies. Poor wee mite! She has all the same affection for these lifeless toys as she would have for live puppies, and sometimes she will not let anybody touch them, not even her mistress. This state of affairs is most pathetic, for sometimes such a bitch is full of milk. She should be taken off all milky fluids, and the sooner

the toys can be removed the better. Give Epsom Salts intern-
ally and smear the milk glands, up towards the neck, with
methylated spirit and the milk will disappear, as also will her
maternal instincts. Sometimes, however, the condition is harder
to eliminate and a veterinary surgeon's advice will have to
be sought.

It is dangerous to leave two mothers with their puppies, for
should the one become jealous of the other, she will ravage
her rival's puppies. There are, of course, other mothers who
will swap puppies, even feed another's as if they were their
own, and it has been known for a bitch to ravage her own
puppies, but I have never heard of this with a Yorkshire
Terrier. I once owned a Pekingese who did and the veterinary
surgeon explained that it does sometimes happen in all
breeds, the bitch going back to the wild state. Over-excitement
should therefore be avoided at all costs.

It would seem that the mother knows best and will not be
bothered with a puppy that is not going to survive. It has been
known for a puppy to be taken from its mother because she
has neglected it, yet, after an abundance of care and attention
has been given to it, after a short while it has suddenly died.
While there is life there is hope, but with puppies like this it
can be heart-breaking after trying so hard. Usually this kind of
puppy remains very small, its rate of growth very slow, and
even a veterinary surgeon cannot tell why or what is really
wrong with it.

It is a different matter altogether when a puppy is frail
through wrong feeding or neglect, because in the hands of an
understanding and patient person it will very quickly be on its
feet again. Two cases I remember particularly. The first was
that of International Ch. Mr Pimm of Johnstounburn who,
when he was bought by his present owner, was an apparently
dying puppy. The second was my own Ch. Midnight Gold of
Yadnum, whose life, at the age of six weeks, was despaired of
by his breeder. The little chap was so limp that his small head
rolled from side to side. I asked the breeder, 'What are you
going to do with him?'

'Oh, I don't know. What can I do? I can't waste time on him;
I have far too much to do otherwise.'

I straightway said, 'Let me take him home with me and I will see what I can do, but I don't think his condition at the moment gives one much hope.'

He was wrapped in a child's woollen scarf and put into my ordinary-sized handbag, which gives some idea of just how small he was. Away I went, not even knowing if he would be alive when I reached home.

As soon as I arrived home I got a warm woollen rug, placed him in it, and warmed some milk into which I put a few drops of brandy and a quarter of a teaspoonful of Glucodin, and spoon-fed him. I did not think he would live until the time for the next feed, but during the night I gave him another tiny drink of the same mixture. Next morning I gave him a slightly larger quantity, and every few hours during that day. He just lay still in his little bed by the fire; that was all he wanted—warmth and a tiny drop of nourishment.

I gave a little larger quantity when I noticed signs of his surviving, and after a day or two there was a decided improvement. At this time my veterinary surgeon had occasion to call at my house to examine a dog who was going abroad, so I showed him the puppy, and he said, 'Well, knowing you, I expect he will have a good chance, but he is very weak.'

Time went on and when the puppy had attained the age of three months the vet happened to call again. I let the puppy walk into the room.

'Oh!' he said. 'What a lovely puppy!'

'Yes, he is, isn't he? Hasn't he grown into a nice puppy?'

'But this is not the one I saw about eight weeks ago?' To which I answered, 'Yes.' He could not believe it.

As his name implies, the puppy became a champion and that before he was two years of age. A Yorkshire Terrier is a tough guy.

To what age can a bitch be bred from? This is a question that is often asked and is debatable. Some bitches will have two or three litters of a fair size and then, no matter how many times they are mated, do not conceive again. I suppose the answer to this is that there is only a small amount of seed to develop. Another bitch will be a prolific breeder, having litter after litter of healthy, strong puppies until she is a ripe old age. I have known several bitches who have produced wonderful litters of five and six healthy, beautiful puppies when in their eleventh year. One, a Yorkie, went astray at the age of fourteen, and successfully reared a litter of five puppies. Fortunately the sire was a tiny dog.

A bitch that does not breed after the first or even the second mating is not necessarily barren. It may be that she is suffering from what is called a nervous womb, and that if her whole nervous system is strengthened the improvement may result in her producing a litter quite normally. It is interesting to note that it is the bitch who determines the number of puppies she is going to produce, for when a bitch, who has in the past had quite good litters, suddenly misses, it is she who has made up her mind she needs a rest.

Should an in-season bitch get out and be mated to a different breed altogether, if taken to a veterinary surgeon straight away, she can be given an injection to prevent any active results taking place. The result will be no puppies, but it is not a good practice, for the results of future matings may be negative. If the misalliance is allowed and the bitch has a healthy litter of puppies, most of them can be taken away from her at birth and destroyed if one desires, but leave the mother one at least, to relieve her of her milk and to give her the joy of having a baby, for the disconsolate mien of a little mother without her family is pathetic to see. Anyway, a pretty cross-bred puppy can be given to a friend or sold for a small amount and the bitch is not considered in the slightest degree less valuable, for breeding purposes, because of the misalliance. She should be treated precisely as she would have been treated had it been a desired mating, and all subsequent litters to a sire of her own breed will be true to type.

It sometimes happens that a bitch cannot have her puppies naturally because the pelvic arch will not expand enough, in which case a caesarian operation has to be performed. Canine surgery makes it possible to save a bitch unnecessary suffering, but most veterinary surgeons do not favour this operation if it can be avoided and will try their utmost to deliver the puppies naturally. The operation need not affect the manner of birth of subsequent litters, and the bitch may have her next litter without any assistance.

After a bitch has left her family some weeks, it is wise to worm her, because all the cleaning up she has had to do must inevitably leave her open to the invasion of these creatures. After this she should return to her usual good health, but some bitches do stay on the lean side for rather a long time. She should be fed with good nourishing food and every effort made to get her back into condition. If she had a large litter and seems fairly worn out let her next heat go by. Give her a well-earned rest; she will repay the next time.

It has been reported that in California, U.S.A., a Yorkshire bitch whelped a second litter of five puppies within eight months, and, the report goes on to state, that whereas this may not be a record for a bitch to have ten puppies within that short period, it is at least quite unusual! It is most unusual and quite abnormal, I would say, and I only hope that the poor bitch was given a good long rest after her ordeal. I have had and known of bitches coming into season three times during a year, but personally I always let the second season pass following a litter. Two litters in a year are quite sufficient for a bitch to contend with, but, of course, I may be thought by some to be much too sympathetic towards my bitches.

6
The Stud Dog

It would seem from the practice of many breeders that they believe with positive certainty that 'like produces like' and have no desire to discuss the subject further.

Some breeders consider pedigree of first importance and mate accordingly, almost entirely ignoring the question of suitability or the fact that even with good pedigrees on both sides the puppies produced are often very poor specimens. They expect that even if the dogs chosen are not themselves all that is desirable, they will be sure to 'throw back' and produce offspring that will resemble ancestors which were good.

Other breeders believe that success at shows is a guarantee of all the most desirable qualities. They invariably seek sires among prize winners without thought to fitness or questioning whether they won in good company or not.

They just think 'like produces like' and 'breed always from the best', the best being those of visible merits irrespective of the qualities of the ancestors, or of conformity of the individuals selected.

Both systems are occasionally successful. Breed to the best, is of course a golden rule, but the family history must also be considered. Those who want to improve their dogs, by developing their most valuable qualities and fortifying them with others, are they who seek the dog that is most likely to correct the faults of the bitch and at the same time preserve the good qualities for the offspring. Admirable qualities must have existed for many generations in order to render their permanency.

Every beginner should start out with the fixed purpose of breeding, not for monetary gain, but to advance the breed to a higher grade of excellence.

The bitch is, of course, a most important element, but a good dog and a well-bred but rather indifferent bitch may breed the very best. In fact, there is reason to believe that a fair proportion of winners have been from bitches that could not win at shows themselves.

It is a mistake to use a dog at stud until he is at least ten months old, and then if possible he should be put to an experienced bitch. The second mating for the dog should not be until he is over twelve months old. This restriction pays in the long run, for the dog is not really fully matured at ten months and his virility and stock-getting ability will last longer if it is not overtaxed when he is too young. On the other hand, if you have kept a puppy to carry on the good work of his sire, and when he has become an adult he is not interested in the opposite sex, do not give up hope, for some mature much later in life than others. My own beautiful and virile stud Graham of Yadnum did not sire a litter until he was nearly three years old; but from that time on, and until he died at eleven years of age, he never refused to serve a bitch, and his progeny have been prize-winners from the start. His son, Beau Brummel of Yadnum, was turned eighteen months before he started. The saying that no two dogs are alike is demonstrated in studs.

Some breeders boast of having so many bitches to their stud; quite a good thing financially, but lacking the good results that puppy producing gives.

A breeder in a small way would be well advised not to keep a male dog unless there is a place well away from his quarters to house the bitch during her period of season.

As time goes on, and one has learned a great deal about the breed, and has the desire to keep a stud dog, then the greatest thought should be given to his selection. A higher standard of perfection should be desired in a dog used for breeding since he may be responsible for many litters in a year, and a bitch only one or two at the most.

A stud dog is valuable to the owner using him for his own bitches, but unless the dog is patronized at stud, he will not earn his keep. Preferably he should be one that can win at Championship Shows, one who is a capable and virile stud dog and who can transmit his characteristics to his progeny.

Dogs who could not be shown have sometimes proved good sires because they have the gift of passing on virtues inherent in their breeding. On the other hand, plenty of sensational winners, and even dogs who have been made champions, have proved most disappointing as sires, and their progeny seldom seen on the benches. The virtue of a dog at stud is shown by the average quality of his progeny from various litters.

An experienced brood is ideal for the first mating. The experience of a bitch willing to help gives a young dog confidence in himself, and afterwards, with bitches not so easy, he will know what is expected of him. A really good stud never refuses. A good plan in training a young stud dog is to let him know that the bitch will be held during the service; but try not to interfere with him too much. Some resent interference while others do not mind a little help.

First try to discover if the bitch to be mated is pleased to meet her mate. If she will flirt with him this kind of mating is usually a happy one. As soon as the bitch shows she is willing to stand, place her on a table—some prefer to keep her on the floor, but oh my, what a back-aching job!—and hold her as firmly as possible, slightly raising her at the back to make it easier for the dog to penetrate. See that the dog has something firm to stand on. Sometimes the stud is very much smaller than the bitch so packing has to be placed under him to let him stand on, so that he is at the right level for his job. If the owner is present, he can hold the bitch's head, and steady her. Sometimes a little vaseline inserted into the vulva is helpful and will make the entry easier. If after prolonged trying no entrance is made, examine the bitch for an obstruction. This is done by first thoroughly cleansing the hands and seeing that the finger to be used has a nail as short as possible. Cover the finger with vaseline and insert into the vulva, but without using force. If it is just a stricture (which is a closing of the passage) this part can easily be opened. If the obstruction is farther up in the passage, then, of course, a veterinary surgeon must examine the bitch. I had a bitch come to one of my studs to be mated, but no matter how hard the stud tried, entry could not be made although the bitch was just ready. On examination by a veterinary surgeon it was found that a large obstruction was preventing an entry, and an operation had to be performed.

Some maiden bitches are very snappy and would bite their mate. With such a bitch it is advisable to have help, for the head must be held firmly so that she cannot possibly turn to bite, or even attempt to, since a stud may often be put off by this action, and time is wasted while he recovers his hurt pride.

Sometimes a maiden bitch, although just right for mating, will forcibly resent the dog, but will react differently towards him if she is left alone for some hours. That same day or the following day try again, when an effective mating will probably result. If her season is on the wane or passed, however much patience you have she will never be mated. Never force a mating; it is all against Nature and is seldom successful.

It is imagined by some that a bitch will not conceive unless a tie has taken place. This is quite a mistaken idea. Many an untied mating has produced a very good litter. The sperm from the dog has only to enter the vagina and the action of the bitch will draw it up into her body. The owner of the stud, however, prefers each mating to result in a tie. The meaning of a tie is that the dog and bitch become firmly united. Hold the dog firmly for a few minutes; he will then try to turn; take the hind leg nearest to you and, still holding him firmly, put it over to the other side of the bitch, and the two will then be back to back.

Do not let the bitch sit down, roll over, or jerk or fidget. If the two cannot be managed, get help and see to it that the bitch is held quite firmly. The dog can be injured and a rupture may result if the bitch is unruly. When the tie is effected it may last anything from ten to even forty minutes. It is a tiring business, and to avoid a backache, have the dogs on a convenient table at which one can sit afterwards and wait.

Two services are not necessary if the first one has been successful. If, of course, the first tie was brief or no tie at all, or it has been arranged beforehand, then a second mating should occur on the following day or the day after that but no later.

After the mating, it is best that the bitch rests if she is not returning with her owner. Leave her in a quiet kennel or in her own travelling-box for a few hours, and place a dish of fresh drinking-water for her.

The dog can now go to his own quarters or into the garden; he often wants to relieve himself. Give him a raw egg beaten up in a little milk and then he will rest. Do not give a meal for at least two hours before a stud dog is to be used, otherwise he will vomit it.

A valuable stud dog needs very special care at all times, and during his matings his comfort and convenience must be considered before the bitch's. He has his reputation to maintain and unless his sexual undertakings are made a pleasure to him he may possibly cool off.

Yorkshire Terrier stud dogs are on the whole quite little gentlemen and do not bother with the bitches in the kennel when they are uninteresting; but when the time comes for one of the bitches to be isolated do it as soon as possible so that the little stud does not get over-excited, working himself up unnecessarily and lessening his stamina for when the right time arrives.

Stud fees should be paid at the time of mating. This fee is for the services of the dog irrespective of whether puppies result from the mating or not. Most owners of stud dogs willingly give a free service if the bitch should miss, but this is not compulsory. I always give a certificate of mating and add to it the day of the mating, the estimated date of birth of the puppies, and a statement that if there are no puppies a free service will be given.

Sometimes the owner of a stud dog may agree to take a puppy from the litter in lieu of stud fee. This arrangement should be given in writing, the exact age when the puppy is to be taken, the sex of the puppy and whether it is to be the first or the second choice of the litter. For the owner of the bitch this is not a profitable arrangement, for the value of a well-reared puppy, especially in these days, is twice if not more than the average stud fee.

The sale of a puppy is sometimes delayed by the failure of the stud's owner to make his choice, or through not collecting the puppy on the appointed date. This is often very inconvenient to the breeder, for the chosen puppy may be the only one left. He then becomes a liability to the breeder, the puppy not being his property, so do try to keep your word.

In issuing the pedigree it should, to make it accurate, include the pedigree to three or four generations, the dog's Kennel Club registration number, and the Kennel Club Stud Book number, if any.

7

Puppy-rearing

People who have never seen a litter of Yorkshire Terrier puppies soon after birth are astonished to find that the little ones are almost all black with a tiny touch of tan above the eyes and a little at the tip of the feet. They resemble very much tiny baby seals, shining and silky. Some years ago I heard of a breeder, who had just started breeding Yorkshire Terriers, destroying a whole litter because he thought his bitch had gone astray, the black puppies being so utterly different from the parents.

All Yorkshire puppies are born with long tails. The tail should be shortened when the puppy is four or five days old. Only if you have a weak puppy and on your vet's instructions should it be left any later. A guide to the amount to cut off is to remove two thirds, leaving one third on, or on the underneath of the tail leave one joint covered with black hair at the end of the tan hair. There are moves to prevent docking by law and you must check if legislation has been passed making this illegal. The operation is not a painful one. The tail is tied with a strong thread above the part to be cut, left for a short time in order to stop the blood-flow into the tip of the tail. The surplus portion can then be removed with a pair of sharp, sterilized scissors, without loss of blood. Dew claws, should there be any, can be removed at the same time. Do not cut too deeply into the flesh as this will cause bleeding, and dab with a little friar's balsam. These operations should be done when the mother is away to avoid causing her unnecessary anxiety.

As the puppy grows, the black fur on the legs gradually disappears and they become all tan. On the head, too, the tan can be seen coming across from ear to ear until in time the whole head will be covered with tan fur. The body-coat starts to shade the correct steel-blue from the neck first, and then all down the spine to the tail, which usually remains a darker shade than the rest of the body. The black tip will remain at the end of the coat for some time and will eventually break off. It is quite fascinating to watch the changing colours of the Yorkshire, for there are few breeds that change so much from puppy to adult.

It has been said by many breeders that they can pick the best puppy in a litter at birth. There is much truth in this as regards colour and shape, but the smallest in a litter can quite well be the largest when mature, or setbacks in rearing may make a 'certainty' an 'also ran'. All in all, however, with common sense and unceasing attention to detail, every puppy has the same chance of success, remembering that the Yorkshire Terrier is one of the hardiest of the toy breeds.

Beginning from the time of birth, a warm temperature should be maintained, and artificial heat used whenever

Tail in right position

Tail too gay

needed. Puppies must be kept very warm as their powers of resistance are invariably low. Warmth is even more essential than food. Between meals and playtime a lot of sleep is absolutely necessary and no puppy will sleep contentedly if it is at all cold. To snuggle into a warm blanket is a joy. When puppies are born in the winter when there is very little sun-shine, an infra-red lamp can be used quite successfully, but do not let the rays come in direct contact with the puppies.

Yorkshire puppies, unlike the flat-faced toys, are especially easy to feed after leaving their mother. By using two saucers, one placed upside down and the other with the food in it placed on top, they will eat without putting their feet in the food and upsetting the lot.

To start with, small meals should be given, four a day with intervals of about four hours. It is most important that meals should be given regularly. Cow's milk is not rich enough unless another food is added. As a matter of interest the milk of a bitch has a high percentage of fat, 9.2 per cent as compared with cow's milk which has 3.7 per cent. The percentage of sugar is 3.1 in the bitch's milk but 6.3 in the cow's. Although the percentage of sugar is higher in cow's milk the lower fat content needs to be supplemented to make it suitable for weaning. Goat's milk is excellent, but it is difficult to obtain unless you live in the country.

At the age of six weeks a puppy should have left its mother and be well advanced in lapping, and even by so young a puppy a varied diet is appreciated: Robinson's cereal, or baby food. Do not make it too thick at first, but gradually increase the consistency and the amount as the puppy grows. Add a little honey or Glucodin to sweeten. Honey is a really good food for all young stock. A raw egg, beaten well, and added to a little warm milk, ground rice pudding, egg custard or a little sponge cake soaked in milk are all enjoyed and are very nourishing.

A few drops of Callo-Cal D can be added to one of the meals. This will strengthen the puppy and will regulate the action of the bowels. Do not forget the cod-liver oil or halibut liver oil; two drops of either to each puppy with the midday feed.

SUGGESTED DIET SHEET

8 a.m. Some baby cereal or one of the milky drinks mentioned.

12 noon. A little very finely chopped cooked meat, broth brought to the boil and poured over some crushed rusks, or small biscuit meal. Saval No. 1 is very suitable, plus two drops of cod-liver or halibut liver oil for each puppy.

4 p.m. A milky drink, milky sweetened tea or the like and a little sponge cake.

8 p.m. The main meal of finely chopped meat, a little more than that given at the noon meal, a little raw, scraped carrot, a pinch of chopped cabbage or parsley.

For a Yorkshire puppy milk must be the principal food during the first months after weaning. Add it to brown breadcrumbs, a little well-cooked rice or any of the baby foods. Feed only a very little and often is the rule, lengthening the time between each meal as the puppy grows.

It is desirable to keep the weight down, but it must be realized that the animal foods, milk and meat, either by themselves or when combined with substances, tend to produce firmness of flesh with an absence of superfluous fat, while, on the other hand, vegetable foods, and particularly starches, tend to fatten, but the combination of the two makes an excellent diet.

An undernourished puppy is an unhappy sight. A puppy must grow to be healthy and it is very unwise, as some breeders do, to give insufficient food or the wrong diet in order to keep the puppy small and light in weight. I heard of a person who weaned a litter of puppies on just brown bread and butter with a drink of tea. The brown bread and butter was quite good in its way, but growing puppies need meat and other vitalizing foods. It was not surprising that one puppy died suddenly.

Over-feeding is, of course equally bad. Never give too much; all puppies are naturally greedy and ever ready for more. If a puppy shows signs of being pot-bellied, has a discharge from the eyes and rubs its behind on the floor, worms are the cause. Most puppies have roundworm which is quite easy to get rid of. Puppies sometimes have tapeworm. This is unusual, but if the dam is infested she will pass them on, hence the importance of worming her before she has her mating. There are many preparations available for the worming of puppies. I prefer tablets supplied by my vet. The dosage is worked out on the puppy's weight and is easily administered. There do not appear to be any signs of distress and the dosage is repeated after ten days, then regularly as directed during the next few months.

About eight weeks is the time to give the puppies names, and feeding-time offers the best opportunity for teaching them. Give each puppy a separate plate when feeding, call one by his name, and when he comes take him and place him in the kennel or in a separate place to have his meal without interruption. When he has finished take him out, call the next one and proceed in the same way. They very quickly begin to know their names and the handling involved gives them confidence and they will come when called.

From the age of eight weeks onwards the teeth will be coming through nicely and a rusk of the kind I have mentioned in another chapter, or a Ryvita biscuit can be given. Both are very good for the teeth and will keep the puppy amused for a long time.

Puppies are inclined to pick up anything they come across, so watch carefully and see that nothing that can be harmful is left about. They have a marked liking for cinders and small pieces of coal which, if swallowed, will cause an upset stomach at least, perhaps something far worse. Any foreign substance swallowed can cause trouble, but since it is only natural for them to try their teeth out on anything, provide a good hard shin-of-beef bone. This can be washed and used time and time again and makes an ideal teething-ring and plaything.

During the process of teething the ear carriage of a Yorkshire puppy very often changes. Even one who has had erect ears from birth will drop them, or carry them in an odd position. They usually recover the correct carriage when teething has finished. Ears should not be tampered with at too young an age. If the leathers are firm, the ears usually need little persuasion to become erect. Massage the leather, between the thumb and index finger, from the base to the tip of the ear. This massage invigorates the blood into the tip and helps to strengthen the muscle. Keep the hair that grows over the edge of the leather cut to the shape of the ear. Any extra weight helps to bend them down.

The ears should be well up between the age of six to eight months, but they sometimes need assistance. A good method is to take as much hair off the leather as possible, cover the whole surface, both the back and front of the ear, with collodion, which can be bought at any chemist's shop, at the same time holding the ear in the correct position until the solution is perfectly dry. This will take a few minutes, but when dry there is no discomfort to the puppy and the collodion will gradually wear off. In the meantime the puppy will have got used to carrying his ears in the correct position, the muscle will have been strengthened, and the final result will usually be a nice erect ear.

Another method is to take all the hair off the ear, then, holding the ear in the correct position, fold it to form a funnel into which the little finger or a pencil can be inserted, thus ensuring a free passage of air into the ear. Now take a piece of one-inch adhesive tape, and, starting at the base of the ear, wind it round until the tip is reached. Do not use too much tape, otherwise the extra weight will be more inclined to weigh the ear down than help to keep it erect. Leave the tape on for a week or more and if it does not come off on its own, an application of surgical spirit will help in removing it. If after a week the ear is still not erect, remove the tape and try again.

Although puppies are not like plants, absolutely dependent for their growth upon the rays of the sun, they share with all Nature its beneficent influence, and when kept constantly in places from which it is shut out they never thrive as they ought and are prone to disease.

Fresh air, sunshine, exercise, and lots of sleep are all equally as essential as good food. Before each meal is the best time to play, and after meals there should be undisturbed sleep. The greatest tonic for them is sunshine, but do not let direct sun-rays fall on the 'tinies' under three weeks, as the eyes cannot yet bear the light. When the weather is fine, a two-months-old puppy should be allowed a run in the garden if possible, for he needs to stretch his legs and expand his lungs and by so doing will get an appetite and sleep well. He should not be allowed to jump from heights, for the bones are still soft and pliable and any jar on the shoulders tends to throw their elbows out. Any injury at this young age may leave the puppy with a permanent disability.

If you haven't a separate room in which the puppies can play and have their freedom on a wet day, an ordinary child's playpen makes a good substitute. There they will be out of harm's way, and the pen can be put in the garden on fine days. The exercise ground for the puppies should, preferably, comprise grass and gravel. Grass alone is altogether too soft, but by exercising on the gravel it will harden the puppy's tiny feet, get them up on their toes, strengthen the pasterns and file down the claws. Always provide a little shade, and a raised platform, with a rug, on which the puppies can rest.

A tummy chill caused by being allowed to rest when still damp after a run on wet grass, or being allowed to lie in a draught, will often result in diarrhoea, which can be very distressing. A little well-cooked rice in milk, or a little sweetened arrowroot, or the white of an egg beaten in a little boiled water will help. If it persists, give a few drops of chlorodyne in a little water.

Here again feeding plays a big part. Now that he is running around he will need a little extra food. By receiving adequate body-forming foods at regular times and by being kept warm, he should never have a day off-colour and should always be full of fun.

Toys of some sort should be provided. Puppies look upon them as their own and carry them into their beds. A good toy is a knitted one, the shape of a man containing a bell or something that will rattle when it is shaken; pad out the shape with cotton-wool. The fun that can be got from such a toy is amazing and puppies will play with them for hours.

A piece of knotted, strong material is also a good plaything, the puppies all joining in a game of tug-of-war. A very hard rubber toy, especially one that squeaks, is another good toy, but here I must stress the importance of taking it away from them as soon as it shows signs of splitting. Puppies think it good fun to pull things to pieces, but a small piece of rubber if swallowed could very easily cause a lot of trouble.

When the puppies are too young to send out into the garden to be clean, or if one lives in a flat, the best way to encourage the clean habit they acquired when with the dam is to spread a good supply of newspaper in a corner or a convenient place. A new treatment for getting puppies to use the same place each time they relieve themselves is made by the Ashe Laboratory and is called 'Puppy Trainer'. A few drops of this liquid on the paper and the puppy will use that spot. When the puppy is old enough to go out into the garden, the paper can be taken to the door that leads out into the garden and a few drops of the 'trainer' put on it as you proceed into the garden. The puppy will soon know what is expected of him. I have tried out this method and found it very successful. With this, as everything connected with puppy-rearing, patience is the one essential.

At six weeks, earlier if you wish, a puppy should be groomed as described earlier, on page 39.

While the puppies are with the dam, she will keep them clean, but during the first weeks after weaning they get sticky with food, and you should expect to have to give a puppy his first wash between the age of eight and ten weeks. Take the puppy, and with the left hand support it under the chest. Continue to do so all through the operation. It will give him confidence, for he may be a bit scared at first. Place him in a shallow bowl of warm water, soak the body and legs, but leave the head until last. The shampoo should be made either of good, pure soap or a well-known canine shampoo, and should be rubbed lightly into the skin, taking care when washing the head that none of it enters the eyes or ears. (A little cottonwool in the ears will prevent any water getting in.) Rinse well in clean, cool water and dry thoroughly. Now brush with a soft brush. The damp will come up again, so be very careful to keep him warm, and when he is thoroughly dry and relaxed give him a small drink of warm milk. Afterwards let him sleep; he will be very tired after his first wash.

When the puppy is about four months old, start his training by walking him on a lead. Some are really wonderful, running along as if they had always been used to it, while others are most trying, wriggling, squirming and almost strangling themselves. It is not always the timid ones that do this. Often it is the forward one of the litter who resents the lead. A good plan is to put the collar on the puppy to let him get used to it. Let him run around in it and he will soon forget that it is there. A little petting, telling him he is a good dog, will all help when the lead is attached to the collar. A lot of patience and a tit-bit will sometimes work the trick. Get him to walk a little and then give him a piece of meat or something he really likes, he will then associate the two and will soon know that when he has his collar put on he is going for a walk and that afterwards he will get a tit-bit.

If a puppy has to be taught to go on a lead in the street, try to choose a quiet street the first time. When a car approaches, watch the puppy carefully. If he seems in any way scared, pick him up, pat him, talk to him to reassure him and then put him down again. He will soon get used to the noises.

It is very unkind not to train a puppy to go on a lead, for a promising youngster who may change ownership at, say, eight or nine months of age, and who has never felt a collar round his neck, is in for an unpleasant time and may never turn out to be the good proposition that his external appearance promised. A show dog will never do well at a show if he will not show. He may easily not take to his new owner, feeling that he is being made to do something he has not had to do in the past and resenting it, for dogs *do* think.

If you are in the unhappy position of having to hand-rear a litter, you must possess the greatest of patience and must have a lot of time if you are to do the job well. You cannot rush the little necessary things that must be done with unfailing regularity, because it is the little things that are so important.

Before I talk about the actual feeding of puppies I must refer to the various jobs that need to be done either before or after meals. After each feed each puppy must be massaged around the rectum with a piece of old, soft linen or cottonwool to encourage natural evacuation. The vagina of the bitch or the sheath of a dog should be gently massaged to cause the passing of water. Should a puppy be constipated, a piece of pure soap shaped to the size of a thick match-stick, gently inserted into the rectum and held there for a short time, will very often have the desired effect. If the passing of water is retarded, a warm flannel held just above the sheath of a dog and the vagina of a bitch will encourage the normal action.

Have a cosy box with a well-wrapped hot-water bottle in it. This is to be the bed and has to take the place of the bitch. The heat of her body will be greatly missed so it is essential that the box should retain the heat. Well line it with brown paper, then newspaper, and add a warm woolly rug.

Gather together all the utensils: saucepan, measuring spoon, thick pottery mug, cotton wool, syringe, towel, vaseline, unscented talcum powder. You will have already purchased one of the milk preparations made for nursing bitches. This is also suitable for rearing puppies; the one I use is made by Sherleys, but there are others. Directions for mixing the milk will be found with the tin and you will need to work out how much your puppies require. If you mix the powder with the warm water in the mug, then place this in hot water in the saucepan; it will keep warm until you require to use it. Take the syringe, making sure it has been thoroughy sterilised first, draw the required amount of milk into it (the quantities are marked on the side of the syringe) and gently place the nozzle to the puppy's mouth. Generally the pressure on the lips will cause the puppy to open the mouth far enough to put the nozzle inside.

If the puppy is reluctant to open up, put your finger and thumb on either side of the jaws and gentle pressure will make the jaw open. The nozzle is hard compared with the nipple of a bitch, but if he is hungry he will soon get used to it and will even start to suck at it. By pressure on the plunger, liquid will be forced into the puppy's mouth, small quantities until he has drawn it down. Try to control the flow: quickly will cause him to choke and milk will be forced down his nose; this should be removed as soon as possible. Then start again. This is a time-consuming task, but it is amazing how quickly the puppy gets the idea.

Feeds are given every two hours for the first two weeks, then the period between feeds is extended and by the time the puppies are more than five weeks old you may get four hours' sleep. If you only have two puppies it isn't too bad, but more than that will mean that by the time you have completed the feed and cleared up you will be thinking about the next one. After the feed is completed carefully wipe the mouth clean of any milk; if this is allowed to dry it will become hard.

Then start on his body functions. With the cotton wool, put pressure on the penis or vulva and the puppy will release urine. Likewise pressure on the rectum will cause the bowels to work. Clean all the areas, put a little vaseline on the rectum and using a small amount of talcum powder dry up any wetness but remove any surplus powder. If you have a bitch able to look after the puppies this is ideal, for she will do the cleaning-up for you.

In some cases when the bitch has eclampsia she will not be able to feed the puppies. If she will mother the puppies you can make her a body stocking to prevent the puppies sucking at the nipples. The sleeve taken out of an old cotton cardigan is ideal. Take the cuff, place it over the bitch's head, then cut two holes for the front legs to come through, but first making sure that the longest part of the sleeve is under the tummy of the bitch. When the legs are through the holes stretch along the body and thread through between the hind legs and turn up on the back. Affix with a large safety pin. It will now be seen that the tummy and the nipples are completely covered. If the sleeve is well stretched the puppies will not be able to get inside. Cut off any excess length. If you can make two one will always be clean.

A few drops of cod-liver oil added to the feed helps growth and assists the functions of the body. Watch the stools of the puppies. They should be firm; if they are of a greenish shade or have a curdled appearance, the digestion is upset. In that event give them a few drops of Milk of Magnesia and a little white of egg beaten up in a little boiled water at the next feed.

Hand-reared puppies will usually start to lap when very young. Here again patience is needed as well as time. See that they do not spill and waste their food or put their feet in the saucer. One can at this time give the puppies a very small amount of scraped raw beef. Scrape the meat off with a spoon; it will be shredded absolutely smooth and can be given to the puppies without fear of their choking because it is like a cream and is easily swallowed. Place a small amount, about the size of a pea, on the tongue and the puppy will suck it in. The amount can be increased as the puppy gets older.

Environment and Temperament

It must be realized that every canine neurosis takes root during puppyhood at a time when the ego is somehow deprived of expansion and hence cannot defend itself against the highly emotional storms that begin to manifest themselves at weaning-time. Breeders may not know all the scientific explanations for what goes on at this time. Before weaning-time the basic infantile emotions were checked or catered for by the dam in the very milk the puppies suckled, and all instincts except the one to feed remained totally dormant until such milk supply ran out. After that, the picture changes and we can watch individual members of the litter faced with managing his own affairs against a buffeting accorded him by the outside world, sometimes through the wire of his pen.

At first this may amount to sharing food with the other puppies, and later may be replaced by battles with one or more puppies for the remains of their food, if they are communally fed.

Where for some reason it becomes necessary to kennel a puppy separately, then one begins to see personality changes occur as the sole result of environment and from this point all subsequent influences are strong factors affecting temperament. At this time each puppy presents himself with a strong temperament, offering only his instinctive demands for food, recreation, fellowship and love, all of which are to be his, even after being sold to a new owner, and living in new surroundings.

What is going on inside him? I wonder. I think it is this: that all the instinctive trends manifest themselves in wishes, through the gratification of which he will attain happiness, and if frustrated, he will be unhappy.

If we consider just one emotion: fear. Few of us can imagine the intolerable emptiness in the life of a puppy deprived of opportunities to play. If any of us suppose that a puppy is even slightly different from a child, who must have play, we are wrong. Fear in a little dog must not be construed as fright; instead it relates to caution, suspicion or apprehension. 'Afraid' means the uncertainty of the unknown or the inexperienced, or of a repetition of some frightening happening. Hence, a puppy deprived of the chance to test his reaction to the ordinary daily experiences is forced to repress the desire to try to join in the fun, and can only hide from such realities when he is eventually exposed to them, all this tending to weaken the healthy action of the brain.

Each puppy in every litter eventually comes to consider himself the personal property of the one who feeds him. Of course this transference from the dam at weaning-time is a natural and necessary one. If kept in kennels for an unreasonable time infantile group-affection is later replaced by individual rivalry for the owner's attention. If none can be found, then the puppy feels frustrated and he then looks to another puppy on whom to wage war. Thus a situation arises that need never have occurred, for had the puppy found the right surroundings in which to occupy his time, the temperament would have been very different. The new owner may have a few difficult months before this condition can be overcome.

The breeder must, therefore, consider it his personal responsibility to handle each puppy with care, for his adult temperament is being built at this very early age and his whole future depends on him.

8

Exhibitions and Exhibiting

Nearly every breeder of Yorkshire Terriers has the urge to
show his dogs, and it is also the great ambition of non-
breeders who own a really good pet, and who have an eye for a
good dog, to be able to present it in the ring to its best advantage. The thrill of winning with a youngster one has bred and
prepared ready for a show is something only the true dog-
lover can fully appreciate, and it is within the reach of all who
have the health, time, the desire and the right temperament
for it. Dog showing is one of the few sports where the amateur
and the professional start level and have an equal chance
of success.

Unless a dog is registered at the Kennel Club he is not eligible to compete at any show recognized by that club. A
person who has bought a registered dog must have it
transferred to his name before such animal is eligible to be
entered for competition.

The wisest of exhibitors are those who have trained from
puppyhood the dog that is to be exhibited. He must be in
excellent health, alert and happy on a lead and ready to respond to any noises the judge cares to make.

The essential in entering a dog for a show is to make sure he
is in absolute show condition. A puppy who has been trained
in all the essentials will not mind what he is asked to do, and
will take to the ring like a veteran. The puppy who has to be
taught in a very short time those things that in the usual way
take weeks or months is not such a good proposition. He will
hate the show and everything appertaining to it. So start early
if you have a very promising youngster by going over the
routine every day.

Ch. Deebees Gold Penny

Ch. Yorkfold Wrupert Bear

Ch. Maritoys Midnight Rose

Ch. Wykebank Tinkerbelle

Ch. Shianda Royal Fanfare

Ch. Naylenor Magic Moment

A bowlful of puppies

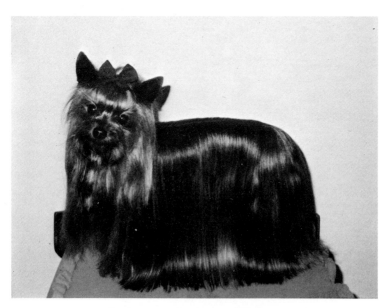

Ch. Azurene Corduroy of Yadnum

Actual Preparation for a Show

Clean the teeth and see that as many puppy-teeth are removed as possible.

The ears are very important. If they are not kept perfectly clean, canker may occur; this is an irritating complaint which often makes the dog put his ears down or his head on one side. To clean the ear, take a matchstick, light it, and with the finger, take off the charred part; it leaves a rounded end. Roll a little cotton wool on this end and dip it in a canker lotion, or a pure oil, and gently insert it into the ear, taking great care not to delve too deep or hard, as the structure of the ear is delicate and can be easily injured. It is astonishing how dirty the ears can get. Trim the fur to the shape of the leather.

Trim the fur around the feet and see that the nails are not long enough to cause discomfort. If they are the dog may walk with a limp, or a hop.

Try to get all these necessary items done well in advance of the date of the show, then the dog will have forgotten all the unpleasant beauty preparations.

Let him see as many different people as possible. Let him be handled, and if he greatly objects to his mouth being looked at, examine it as many times as possible, making a game of the action, so that he will not mind the judge examining his mouth to see that the teeth are even and the formation of the jaw correct.

The majority of show dogs are kept in oil and the hair tied up. The usual way is to use tissue paper, about two inches wide, and of the length required to take in all the hair. Place a small amount of hair in the paper which should be folded so that the hair is covered, and then turn upwards from the bottom, over and over until the top is reached, then tie it. The fall, or the top-knot, is done in the same manner, also the moustache. Very fine linen or silk can be used instead of tissue paper.

Before a show, therefore, the dog must be washed twice to ensure that all the grease is out of the coat. Use a good shampoo or soap as recommended in another chapter. If the coat is very long, it is essential that it should not be broken. By rubbing it dry with towels this can very easily happen, the hair being so fine. To avoid this soak as much of the water out of the coat with a wash-leather and then brush well in front of a warm fire until quite dry. If you possess a hair-dryer use this, but do not let the heat come in close contact with the skin, and do not use this method if the dog is very nervous of the machine.

Some people never rub the long coat at all even while bathing; they just use a brush. This method keeps the coat the right way; it also keeps it from tangling. Wet the dog all over, pour a little shampoo on the coat and, with the brush, gently go up from the base of the hair to the spine, with the same movement that you use when the coat is dry. Hair never tangles from the root, so whether wet or dry always start at the base and work up to the spine.

Examine the anal gland; squeeze it between the thumb and finger with a piece of cotton wool, and the mattery substance will be evicted, thus making the dog feel much more comfortable. The secretion of this matter is often the cause of a dog going lame, something one does not want to happen.

When the dog is thoroughly dry his hair, if long, should be tied up again, but on no account should it be tied if it is not absolutely dry otherwise it will hang in lovely waves, which is quite wrong, for a Yorkshire's coat should be perfectly straight. Some dogs look their best when washed the day before a show, but with others it is better to wash a few days before to let the coat settle down. It all depends on the nature of the hair.

Get everything ready: the pass, ribbon, lead, food, drink, brush and comb, a bottle of diluted T.C.P., newspaper, pen curtain and cover for show case, and a rug. Try to give as much time and thought to doing all the essential preparations the day before the show, and then when you are ready to start you have not to wonder 'Have I got everything?'

It is a sound idea for the owner of a good dog who wishes to show him to enter him in an Open Show, or a Members' Show, where the breed is scheduled, and see how he behaves. Some are born showmen, others need the patience of Job practised on them before they gain confidence in the ring, and some never make a show dog, being always in too nervous a state.

Exhibiting

Try to have self-confidence and your dog will react to your feelings. A dog good enough must, in the end, be recognized, but if his owner or handler is nervous the dog will most certainly be the same, thus spoiling his chances, for however well a dog looks, if he will not walk or make the most of himself, he loses points.

At some Open Shows, and most General Championship Shows, benches are provided to house the dogs while at the show. Do get your dog used to being shut up in a similar pen or if preferred his own travelling case or basket. The sight of a little one penned for the first time, and then left, is pathetic; what with barking and yapping he gets worn out and becomes a great nuisance to those benched nearby.

Do not enter in too many classes at first. Get used to showing and, as time goes on, experience will be gained and many lessons learned. If your dog wins well when first you show him, he will, of course, be handicapped and will be exempt from competing in lower classes at later shows; so always, before entering your dog's details on the entry form which is with the schedule provided by all canine societies, carefully read the definition of classes. It is very easy to enter your dog in a wrong class and by so doing you will have to forfeit your prize money (if any) and will be most disappointed.

Veterinary inspection is now not compulsory at the entrance to a show—but, should you be advised in the schedule that there will be a veterinary inspection prior to entry to the show, this is usually carried out at the entrance and your exhibitor's pass is stamped 'passed by Vet'. Make your way into the hall and find out where you are benched. If your dog is going to occupy the bench provided, it is usual not only to make the pen look attractive, but also to make the occupant cosy; to hang a curtain on the inside of the pen; put brown paper or newspaper on the floor and a nice warm rug,

one that the dog is used to is preferable. If he knows the smell
of it he will settle. Before doing all this wipe the sides and floor
of the pen with mild antiseptic. This precaution is taken
against possible infection as one does not know the condition
of the former occupant. It also cleans the pen which sometimes is very dusty, and prevention is better than cure.

Dogs should not be left in their show cases but placed on
display in the pens provided. In warm weather care must be
taken to ensure the dog has enough air and always leave the
front open so that visitors can see the exhibit, that is what they
have paid admission for. When the dog has settled, and if time
permits, go and get a little refreshment if you have not taken
any with you, and buy a catalogue if you have not already done
so.

Sometimes Yorkshires are judged early, and if this is to be so
give your dog a thorough brushing through to see that there
are no waves caused by the tying-up, a straight coat being a
point of the breed. Take with you a small container with either
distilled or rain water in it, to spray on the coat; then brushing
through will help to straighten the coat. This water is pure and
so is not faking. Any preparation added to the coat could be a
form of faking and if this is proven after tests the owner can be
disqualified from showing or attending shows by the Kennel
Club. Any preparation could also apply to any colourant
which is applied to the coat. Tie the top-knot with a good tying
ribbon, preferably of the same colour as his lead.

The number of the ring to be used for judging will be found
in the front of the catalogue.

Before entering the ring try to exercise your dog and if he
relieves himself all well and good. Some will not oblige all day
and just wait until they get home to their own garden. Often
through his not having relieved himself he will act in the most
unusual manner and with the most disappointing results. To
the beginner may I suggest, give all your attention to your dog,
no matter what else is going on. Wait until after the judging,
which is the serious business of the day, before starting to chat
with your fellow exhibitors. They will appreciate it because
they will be concentrating on the preparation of their dogs,
and will not want to be distracted from that.

Find out the time of the judging and be on the alert as to

when your exhibit is needed in the ring. Try to get a ringside seat and watch with keen interest as the judge goes over the other exhibits. Should your dog behave himself well, even if he is not fortunate enough to win a prize, give him a pat or a word of encouragement; he will appreciate it and you will find that show-going will become a pleasure to him.

Never scold him if things do not go quite right or put him into his pen without a word, for, like an elephant, a dog never forgets.

When the class in which you have entered is to be judged the steward will call your dog's number; so do try to remember it and be ready. A steward's work is made so much easier and time is saved if you co-operate as much as possible. Put your ring number in a prominent place on your person so that it can be seen easily by the judge and the steward, or anyone interested.

Stand your dog on his case and think of nothing else but your dog looking his very best. The judge will have him up on the table provided and examine him thoroughly and then he will ask you to walk him. Gently place him on the floor and slip a light-weight lead over his head. Give him a reassuring pat or a quiet word of encouragement and he will trot away with you, thinking how nice to go for a walk and how nice to show off. That is the well-trained dog, but if he will not follow and is inclined to sit down in the ring, do not get cross and tug at his lead, but pick him up and take him to the other side of the ring and see if he will walk that way. Sometimes it comes off, but if there is no improvement and you have a tasty morsel, give him the scent and maybe he will follow, thinking he is going to get it.

When you are told to walk him give him a fair amount of loose lead. Do not hold it too tight, jerking his head up too high and raising him off the ground. Let him walk naturally, keeping him on the side where the judge can see him. A dog is more difficult to show than a bitch; sometimes he will keep his nose fixed to the floor, especially if it has been soiled by a bitch, for some unscrupulous exhibitors will take a bitch to a show when she is in full season, thus exciting all the dogs. In a case like this, try to find a part of the ring where it looks fairly clean, and put the dog on a tight, but not too tight, lead. A fairly good plan is to put a touch of T. C. P. or some such smelly fluid on his nose; he then smells that instead of the dirty floor.

Years ago most Yorkshire Terriers were shown off a lead; they followed to heel, being the only toys privileged to do this. All dogs must be shown on a lead; this is a rule of the Kennel Club. Some years ago a judge insisted that the Yorkshire should be shown on a lead, his explanation being that he did not want the large dogs around to make a meal of one.

When the judge has finished with him, place him on his case again, and while the judge is going over the other exhibits let him sit and relax, but as soon as the judge has nearly finished judging all the other dogs, make him stand up facing the judge. Never let him turn his hindquarters to the judge, for that way the judge cannot see the correct shape. The judge wants to see the front or side view.

Should you be told by the judge or the steward to stand your dog in a certain spot, go exactly where you are told and stay on that spot unless told to move. Remember that the other exhibitors in the ring are there for the same purpose as you, and if by your being thoughtless you stand in front of the exhibit next to you, the judge's view of that dog is obscured, and that can sometimes lead to much unpleasantness. I have often seen it done by exhibitors who should, and do, know better; it is exasperating.

When the final awards are made, whatever they may be, accept them with grace as the judge's decision is final. The dog who wins today might go cardless tomorrow.

At a show you primarily desire an expert's opinion on your dog; secondly you would like to be in the prize money. Even if your dog was at the end of one class, he might be much higher placed, or even first, in the next, so never show your disapproval of the judge's decision by leaving the ring or by tearing up an award card; it is a great insult to the judge. There are only three money prizes: first, second, and third, so if at first you are not successful do not give up, but work on your dog and he will reward you.

Sit at the ringside and try to emulate the methods of other exhibitors, some being past-masters of the art of successfully showing a Yorkshire Terrier. Your dog may have all the qualities of those who have beaten him, but if he is not presented as well as the others he loses on general appearance.

When all the judging is finished the first thing to do is to give him a small drop of diluted T.C.P. to drink—one drop to five of water. Then wipe him underneath, giving an extra soaking to the pads of his feet. Then put him in his pen, give him some refreshment, a drink of fresh, clean water or milk if he prefers it, but do not leave him alone for a while. Your being there will help him to enjoy his meal and settle down for a quiet snooze; you can then have some refreshment yourself.

The T.C.P. acts as a safeguard against contamination. Many dogs may have been in the ring before yours and prevention is better than cure. Some few years ago the T.C.P. caravan was always at the main shows all over the country and a free service was given, an attendant doing all the various things; spraying the mouth and swabbing the underneath, the dog standing on soaked pads of T.C.P. I always availed myself of this service and am ever grateful to the proprietors of the product, I am only sorry the service had to be discontinued. So my advice is always to have a bottle of five parts water to one part of T.C.P. for the dog to drink, and stronger solution for external application.

It is also a wise plan to have a little brandy or whisky in case of a dog getting a chill, for some of the halls are very cold and draughty in the winter; just a few drops in a little milk will ward off a chill.

For yourself, when possible take a small fold-up stool or a lightweight chair to sit on as seating accommodation is seldom provided by the promoters of the shows to be used at the benches, and one can get so very weary standing about for hours. Sometimes it is impossible to get even a cup of tea or any refreshment, through judging arrangements going haywire: for instance, your breed is timed to be judged in the morning, and hour after hour slips by during which you cannot leave the benches in case the judge is ready. It sometimes happens that a judge is delayed on his journey to the show, or at the last moment cannot keep his appointment, and so another judge has to fill in for him, and maybe the new judge has several other breeds to do before he is free to do yours. All sorts of unforeseen things can happen to hold up judging, so always take a little food and drink for yourself in case you cannot get to the refreshment room, which is usually crowded anyway.

There are some owners who cannot spare the time for preparing and showing their dog, and are justifiably upset, knowing that a perfectly lovely dog in all respects must stay at home. People so situated can still show their dogs by employing what is known as a professional handler, although it is usually a somewhat costly procedure, as the handler must have the dog at his own home for a short time to get to know him, and for the dog to get used to the handler's ways. There is, of course, a scale of charges for the service, but the owner is spared the expense of attending the show. The time factor may come into it also. An inexpensive way out is if one has a friend who is an excellent person in handling the dog in his own house, and able to do it at a show.

In the hands of an expert, a Yorkshire Terrier may remain in show condition for years, whereas under wrong treatment he may not last through a whole season. It is scarcely necessary to add that none but people who have some knowledge of the treatment of this tiny toy, and a bountiful fund of patience, should go in for Yorkshires; indeed it has often been said that two Yorkies require as much care and attention as one child, if not more.

When the judging is all over and the time draws near to go home do refrain from the practice of some exhibitors who tie up every hair on the poor dog's body, making him look like a freak instead of the handsome fellow he is. Some visitors, having arrived late at the show, come along to the benches and, on seeing the tied-up dogs, openly make a laughing stock of them, with exclamations like, 'Oh, aren't they funny, poor little things. Fancy being all tied up like Topsy; what's it for? To make its hair curl?'

I know that with the very long-coated Yorkies it is unwise to leave all the coat untied, but do try to limit the amount you tie up until after the show. I am afraid many prospective buyers are put off by this procedure and ask, 'Must I keep my dog like that if I have one?'

'I think it is cruel,' one lady said to me, but I quickly informed her that the dogs preferred to have their long tresses tied up out of the way, and, of course, should you have a Yorkshire Terrier you can keep its coat short by cutting it. The great length of coat is for show purposes only.

9

Judging and Stewarding

The whole system of exhibiting dogs is largely in the hands of the judge, who is a very important person in the canine world. A good judge should know the anatomy of the body and be fully capable of determining what constitutes the best of the breed.

It is his duty to serve the interests of the breed and to promote its progress. He must have an intimate knowledge of the breed, possess integrity, and have the courage of his convictions. A judge who does not exercise this position of trust fairly does much harm and exhibitors distrusting his decisions will, in all probability, not show under him again, thus causing the entries to fall off.

A judge must have complete confidence in his own opinion, so that later if he finds he has put a big winner down, or an unknown up, he will not be afraid of the hostile criticism of the offended. He must possess extensive knowledge of the breed and a clear idea of the technique employed in judging.

A good judge of livestock usually has a natural ability, without which he would never make a good judge. Some can judge any animal on four legs; they seem to have a flair, what is called 'an eye', and can see unsoundness at a glance, as well as quality and style. There has been endless controversy on the subject of the qualifications required by a judge. Some have suggested classes for judges, or aspirants to the rank of judge. This idea is not of much use to the novice, at least, not to my way of thinking, for the simple reason that if the aspirant has the natural ability he will, in due time, become a good judge.

If a person is invited to judge, unless he is fully conversant with the standard of the breed he should not be tempted to accept. By showing good sound specimens himself, he should be capable of seeing, not only the merits of his own dogs, but those of others also.

Few dogs conform to all the standard points, but the best dog present should go to the top. A very long-coated dog may look a most beautiful sight, but after scrutinization by the judge may not be placed at the top, because one or even several bad points have been discovered. A judge should concentrate on his exhibits and be so absorbed in his task that nothing distracts him, and the person leading the dog should not be recognized.

A novice judge might sometimes feel a little embarrassed when having to judge a friend's dog, but if he gives a fair decision on the dog's qualities and his judgement is questioned he should not worry. When judging, one should have no friends, but it is not only the novice judge who makes the mistake of favouring friends.

Before accepting an undertaking to judge, thought should be given to the method to be followed, for anyone acting in this capacity without a worked-out plan can come to grief. One may decide to look for the best in a class first. It will usually be found that first impressions hold good, and very often the ultimate winners are drawn from these. Should one dog not come up to expectations on handling, a substitute can be found from among the less attractive. It is no use working from the bottom upwards.

It is very important to make your procedure intelligible both to the exhibitor and to the ring-sider. While the judge is judging the dogs, the onlookers are judging him, and they are not interested in watching someone standing about and dithering in indecision, nor one who is rushing through his job to get away. Every exhibit, good or bad, is deserving of the same amount of time and examination spent on it.

Do not forget that exhibitors showing their dogs under you are doing you an honour whether you are a young judge or one of long standing.

When reporting on a show, it is necessary to distribute praise and blame fairly. A whitewashed report is of no value, and one that mentions all the faults without giving credit for good points does unnecessary harm to the dog and the owner.

It is your opinion only that decides which dog is best, but such dogs may meet again under a different judge, whose opinion is entitled to as much respect as yours, and the placings may be

Roach back

Correct back

Down at the shoulders

reversed. So do not stress faults too much unless you are fairly sure a reasonably good judge would agree with you. So to young judges, when in the ring, know what you want and try to get it, and never fear the consequence.

Examine the exhibits back and front. It is difficult to assess the merits of long-coated specimens, so extra care must be taken to see if the shoulders are out, or the hind legs too spread, or if the dog is down on the pasterns. A long coat can hide a lot of faults.

Some exhibitors are very clever at concealing bad movement, but they should not pass a judge who knows his job.
Examine the mouth to see that the teeth are as even as
possible.

Take the dog's head in your hands to note the size, the
shape and colour of the eyes, the fineness of the muzzle, the
set of the ears, and the general expression. Lift a foreleg to feel
the bone and examine the feet: white claws are a bad fault. Go
over his back to feel firmness of flesh and condition. Have the
top-knots untied, for a golden top may still be black
underneath.

The important thing is to go over the points of each dog in
the same order; that way you will not miss anything. I have
seen some judges go over large classes most thoroughly, yet
not examine the mouth of any dog or even undo a single top-
knot. I once had the experience of taking a lovely dog, a winner nearly every time shown, to a Championship Show
hundreds of miles from home, and travelling all night to get
there. The judge at the show completely ignored the fact that
mine was the only new dog in a class, although the steward had
informed him, and in consequence the dog was never
examined. This was the most unbelievable behaviour from a
man who was supposedly a good judge.

Some judges find it an easy excuse to eliminate some of the
competitors for having a short coat, but if the conformation of
the body is good, the colour of the coat excellent and all other
essentials of reasonable merit he should, in lots of cases, go far
higher than the dog with a long, bad-coloured coat.

Good texture, density and colour in a coat are discernible
whether its stage of growth is long or short. Its condition on
the day is of only a temporary nature and should not be
allowed to outweigh completely the permanent essentials of
construction, type and colour. The age of a puppy and, in fact,
of all exhibits, should be ascertained. In a junior class, a
puppy exhibited has often to meet dogs of any age up to eighteen months, and some are very near the limit. A puppy of
seven months cannot be expected to have as long a coat as an
older one, and here again colour should play a part.

Having made your decision as a judge, place the first,
second, third and reserve (which is fourth place), mark your

judge's book plainly and sign your name on two of the slips. The steward will then come forward and present the prize cards.

Do not be distracted from your job. It is most annoying to exhibitors to have a judge who leaves the ring to chat with an acquaintance or a friend at the ringside. Not only do the exhibitors get impatient, but the poor dogs, who have been brushed and brushed, are already getting weary. Another don't is, do not at any time during the judging stop have a smoke. Exhibitors are not allowed this privilege and the judge who smokes looks very unbusinesslike, to say the least. The smoke can also get into the dog's eyes.

When all is finished and all the necessary signing of the certificates over, you will in all probability have a few of the exhibitors waiting to have a word with you, about the placings of theirs and other dogs. As far as you can, try to answer the questions so that they enlighten the exhibitor on the reasons for your placings.

Judging is an interesting if thankless task. Try not to go home after your judging appointment and ponder over all the mistakes you think you have made. You have given your opinion and that is all you are supposed to do. What anybody else thinks or says either to your face, or behind your back, should be of no interest to you. It can be very hurtful to have brick-bats thrown at you, but if your job has been honestly done you will in the end be considered a good judge.

There are a few Championship Show judges of some experience who have openly said, 'I make a point of encouraging the novice exhibitor,' or 'I never award both Challenge Certificates to the same owner.' Why? Is he truly judging the dogs? If so, and both sexes are the best of their breed, should they not both be awarded the highest honour?

If the dogs do not come up to the standard of the breed, the judge can withhold the certificates.

A considerate judge should carry out his work quietly and a conscientious one should always keep in his mind the general characteristics of the breed. If he is a breeder he may have stronger leanings towards certain features than others, but in judging he should hold no personal preferences and his only concern should be for the welfare of the breed.

Without judges there would be no dog shows, and judging, because it is a great responsibility, should not be undertaken light-heartedly.

Stewarding

The duties of a steward are varied, many, and not always fully appreciated by either the experienced or the novice. A steward is more often than not taken for granted and little credit is given for a somewhat thankless task. Often he is blamed when it is the exhibitor's own fault that errors are made. An exhibitor is most annoyed if the exhibit misses his class and yet often it is sheer carelessness; quite often the exhibitor cannot be found. Time at a show is valuable, and if every exhibitor is late in the ring, judging would never finish.

A steward is actually an unpaid public servant except that he invariably gets a free lunch, which he rightly deserves. Exhibitors, therefore, should be most grateful for a steward's help and should try to make his task as easy for him as possible.

At most large shows two stewards are in attendance on the judge. Their first obligation is to be at the show in good time, and to report to the secretary's office where they will be given the award cards, ring numbers and a catalogue. They then proceed to the ring to which they are allocated and while awaiting the judge sort out the ring cards and award cards into the proper classes, separating them by a rubber band.

They see that the table, one or two chairs, the award board, on which the award card is hung, some chalk and a duster, and, very necessary, a pail with sawdust and a shovel are provided. By this time the judge has usually arrived and, with everything ready, can start. One of the stewards goes to tell the exhibitors that the dogs are wanted in the first class. Some exhibitors can be very casual, the kind of behaviour that can be very trying. When all the exhibitors are in the ring, and the number cards have been handed out, the judge should be advised of any absentees so that he can mark them in his book.

The stewards now withdraw to the side of the ring but are in readiness should the judge require them.

When the judge has placed his first four dogs, who should then be lined up in the middle of the ring, he will beckon his stewards. One will hand the award cards to the winners, and to the other the judge hands two slips torn from his judging book. One of these is posted or stuck on the award card at the back of the board, and the other is left on the table to be collected by a show official. The numbers of the winners are chalked up on the board for the benefit of spectators and exhibitors who wish to keep a record. All classes are dealt with in the same manner.

The exhibits which appeared in an earlier class are lined up and should be placed in their right order, that is to say, first, second, third and reserve and so on, at the opposite side of the ring to the new exhibits. Exhibitors often wander and stand in a wrong place and this should be noted by the steward.

Actually there is no difficulty about this lining-up, but complications may arise in later classes when two or more dogs, all having won prizes, have not met each other. Make sure to get this right and tell the judge exactly what the position is.

The best of judges have accidentally reversed a decision, but a good steward should be able to prevent such a thing happening. It is the duty of the steward to ensure that every dog is in the ring when wanted, and if one is missing that has not been reported absent, he must go to the benches to see if the exhibit is there. Sometimes the owner is sitting quite unaware that he or she is wanted. If a steward finds the bench empty, he may have to search around to see whether the dog is being exercised. If the dog is on the bench and the owner cannot be found, another exhibitor can show the dog in the owner's absence. This happens quite often when an owner has two different breeds, and they are being judged at the same time. In this case the owner should make arrangements for a friend to show one while he is engaged with the other.

It is rather a worry to a steward if the dogs are benched a long way from the rings, but usually the show committees try to arrange for the rings to be near. A steward should stop exhibitors crowding into the centre of the ring, and with a firm voice tell them to get back; even then, some still do it. Try to make the ring as large as possible; it is much better for the dogs and definitely better for the judge, who wants to see their action when on the ground.

Keep the award cards up to date. A steward, having a first-class view of the proceedings which often is not obtainable from the ringside, can in his own way arrange the dogs as he sees their merits and compare with the judge's. This is a very good way to learn more about the breed, and in time, if he aspires to be a judge, he will enter the ring and feel much happier and more confident than he ever thought he could be.

10

The Pet

Of all the toy breeds there is no finer pet than the Yorkshire Terrier. He is small, strong and hardy, very lovable and fearless. If made one of the family he will know all the moves of every member of the household. He is not a one-man dog; he will show his devotion to all, but maybe the one who feeds him gets a little extra attention.

If you start off with a young puppy his education may begin at a very early age, but efforts must, for the first few months, be largely directed to the cultivation of specific virtues, such as cleanliness, obedience, etc. While aiming to make the exercise of these virtues habitual, bad habits must be anticipated and prevented, if possible. A puppy who has access to a yard or garden soon becomes voluntarily clean. House-breaking should never be thought of during the very cold weather as cleanliness in habit is then out of the question. Give him a definite place to relieve himself and he will always use it, for a puppy shut out in the rain and cold for any length of time can catch a chill.

That he is unclean in his habits is only when his natural tendencies have been prevented by restraint or neglect. He is capable of some understanding at a very early age, but such beastly practices as dabbing his nose in filth and throwing him out of doors should never be indulged in, for he is not quite so understanding at that age, and will grow into a timid little dog.

Being so small, a Yorkie is an ideal pet to have if living in a flat, and when food is an expensive item he is quite an economical one, eating in some cases much less than a cat. What good friends a Yorkie and a cat can become, especially if they are brought up as puppy and kitten together! It is hardly fair to introduce a dog of any kind into the home of an old favourite cat, for jealousy is sure to develop. So make sure the old cat gets more attention than the puppy to start with. They invariably become good friends.

The dog, like the horse, is the friend of man, and a Yorkshire will stick to his master, and guard him to the best of his tiny ability. His loyalty is so whole-hearted that it is sometimes difficult not to idolize, but a good master will not allow himself to go to extremes.

There are some who spoil their dogs so that they become snappy and distasteful to all except their owner, and this is a disadvantage to the breed in general. A lady who contemplated buying a Yorkshire as a pet went up to an exhibitor at a show and, whilst talking to her, put her hand out to pat the dog in the exhibitor's arm. The dog immediately tried to bite her. 'Oh my,' exclaimed the lady, 'I did not think Yorkshires were spiteful, snappy little dogs.' When the incident was partly forgotten, I assured her that it was an isolated case, that most Yorkies were very good-tempered and lovable, and she was persuaded to have one. Mistress and dog lived together, did every possible thing that could be done together and were absolutely inseparable for eighteen years. Like lots of others, when the little dog died, his mistress was so distressed she vowed that she could not possible have another, but as time went by, she was lonely and sought the companionship of another Yorkie and both are quite contented.

The Yorkshire, being a terrier, will enjoy a romp in the garden or a field, and go for very long walks, never seeming to tire.

If scolded for doing something wrong he does not sulk, but will wait patiently for the first opportunity to give some little sign, such as sidling up to his owner, that he is sorry.

Treat him in the same manner as a show dog would be treated as regards feeding, exercise, grooming and sleeping.

If brought up with children, Yorkshires are the greatest of companions and love to join in all the play, although sometimes the urge to keep a ball that has been thrown takes effect. If he is so disposed he will run away every time the children approach him.

He is an excellent house dog; the least unusual noise will make him bark until his owner finds out the cause. When going to a show some years ago, I stopped to buy a newspaper from my agent at the railway station. Seeing the basket, he asked if I was going to a show. I answered, 'Yes.'

'May I see what is in the basket?' So I opened up.

A gentleman buying his newspaper asked if he also could see. 'Oh,' he said, 'a lovely little Yorkshire Terrier, the burglar's enemy. Have you ever noticed,' he went on, 'how at a small hotel or a road-house, a Great Dane and a Yorkshire are kept? The Great Dane attacks the intruder, the Yorkshire, having given the alarm, and being so tiny, can hide under any low furniture. I know, as I am a member of the Criminal Investigation Department.'

Many years ago we had as neighbours a family who owned a beautiful Yorkie named Prince and who moved house to live north of the Thames. The day after their removal we found Prince sitting on the step of the empty house. We fed him and then got in touch with his owner, who came and took him back to his new home. The next day the same thing happened and again his owner came to get him. Going into the empty house to see if anything had been left, Prince made straight for the garden and barked with joy to see his little companion Teddy, a tortoise who had been forgotten in the excitement of moving. How Prince managed to get through all the city traffic was a mystery, for he had miles to cover.

Another little pet was a bitch named Dinah. For four years, she was her mistress's constant companion, only seeing her master occasionally. She was allowed all over the house in the usual way, but one day her mistress's door was closed and try as she would, she was not allowed in. Day after day she sat on the mat outside the door; she left her food and it was quite a difficult job to get her to go into the garden from which she raced back to keep vigil outside the closed door.

At last the door opened and out came her mistress, plus a baby. Dinah almost went mad with joy, but her devotion lost her nearly all her lovely coat. She was absolutely bare in places, but the love and attention of her mistress, and the vet's medicine, soon made it grow again. The veterinary surgeon explained that the loss of the hair was due to a shock to the nerves, caused through anguish at not being allowed to go to her mistress.

There is a book called *Greyfriars Bobby*, written by Eleanor Atkinson, in which she tells the story of a little terrier called

Bobby. He is actually described as a Skye Terrier but by his photograph and the model of him on his memorial outside the Greyfriars Auld Kirkyard, Edinburgh, he is definitely more like a Yorkshire Terrier in shape and general appearance. In Bobby's day of youth, that was in 1858, Queen Victoria lived at Windsor or Balmoral. Bobby became very attached to an old shepherd called Jock, who visited Grassmarket in Edinburgh. Bobby would hunt around for him and follow him to the little restaurant where he dined. The devotion of this little dog to Jock was astonishing and when after many years Jock died, the little dog followed the funeral procession, walking underneath the coffin. He was turned out of the kirkyard time and again, but would return at night and lie under the stone on the grave next to Jock's. This he did for eight years. Bobby was eventually caught by the police and was brought before the Lord Provost, Sir William Chambers, Laird of Glenormiston, charged with having no licence, but the children of the slums who were devoted to Bobby went from house to house and collected seven shillings for a licence, and so Bobby was reprieved from his death sentence.

When it was learned of the devotion of Bobby to Auld Jock, the little dog became a sort of hero. He had a band of new leather with holes in one end and a stout buckle on the other put round his neck and riveted in the middle of it was a shining brass plate, with the inscription which read, 'Greyfriars Bobby, from the Lord Provost, 1867. Licensed', and he was given the freedom of the City of Edinburgh.

The soldiers of the castle tried to hold Bobby as their pet, but he always found his way back to the kirkyard. Bruised and torn after the very steep descent to the town, Bobby, having got away from the castle a second time, died, after his vigil which had lasted fourteen years. He was buried in a grave next to Jock. Queen Victoria, when visiting Scotland, went to see Bobby, Baroness Burdett-Coutts went all the way from London to see him, and it was she who startled the Lord Provost and church officers when she said that Bobby should be buried with his old master.

All the endearing qualities in a dog reach their height in this loyal terrier. Lady Burdett-Coutts had a monument made to commemorate Bobby's devotion.

In the porch of Greyfriars Kirk is a glass case in which are the papers relating to this case and the collar of BOBBY, so if you are in Edinburgh any time why not try and see them?

Tiny, a medium-size Yorkie, loves nothing better than to ride on the bonnet of his master's tractor. How he manages to maintain his hold when the tractor goes over the rough ground nobody knows, but he has never fallen off and always seems to be very happy.

A tiny Yorkshire of mine, weighing only 2¾ lb, a wonderful show and stud dog, acted as our alert during the war. Long before the siren sounded he would be waiting at the entrance of our shelter, for somehow he knew. He lived to be sixteen years of age.

This is not an uncommon age for a Yorkshire. A friend who bought a bitch puppy from me had her as a companion and devoted pet all through the bombing of London. Julie died at the age of eighteen, but this length of life is unusually long for such a small dog. Ten to fifteen years is an average age, although there is on record a Yorkie that lived to be twenty-five.

The life of a pet Yorkshire should be a most enjoyable one and full of fun. He is a joy to be with on walks, playing games or when going for a swim. Some of them just love the water, but you should give him a rinse in fresh water if he has been in the sea, for salt water will make his coat harsh if it is allowed to dry into it.

Do Yorkshire Terriers remember? An adult dog of mine was sold to an American, and he settled down in his new home wonderfully well. Two years later I visited his home and when entering greeted his master and mistress. I then spoke to him, using my old pet name for him. He made one dive at me, greeted me with all the old affection, would not leave me, and came and slept all night on my bed. He is now an American champion.

Many people who have had a dog as a pet nearly all their lives and have changed to a Yorkshire Terrier usually remark that they would never change again to any other breed.

What kind of a mixer is a Yorkshire? This question is often asked. Usually they are very good mixers and various breeds such as a bull terrier and a Yorkie are excellent friends. The German Shepherd and the Yorkie mentioned earlier were inseparable friends. If one anticipates having two different breeds of dogs as pets, try to have them as puppies of about the same age and, for convenience, of the same sex, and let them grow up together. Try not to favour one more than the other, for the result will be jealousy and that, of course, leads to trouble. Two Yorkshires as pets are ideal; they keep each other company when the owner wants to go out and it is inconvenient to take a dog along. When they are puppies they play and amuse each other, but it means spending a lot of your time to keep only one happy.

If you take an older dog as a pet, do try to do everything in exactly the same way as regards feeding, sleeping, exercise and all the little personal things that the dog was used to when with his former owner. If you do, he will soon settle down and with lots of fussing and love will make a delightful little pet.

A Yorkshire is not altogether the silly little dog he is thought to be by some, and it is astonishing how quickly he can adapt himslf.

Training a pet in obedience can be an interesting experience and it is not difficult. Classes are sponsored by various canine associations where dogs of all breeds are trained. To join a class, you must become a member of an association. The dogs meet each week and are put through their paces, and when they are proficient they can compete at the shows in the obedience classes. One little Yorkshire Terrier bitch I knew gained most marks during her training, beating all her big brothers and sisters of such breeds as Boxers, Poodles, German Shepherds, etc. She would go shopping with her mistress, who would leave her outside the shop, tell her to sit and stay, which she would do no matter how many other shoppers gave her a pat or spoke to her. There she would sit until her mistress came out of the shop and taking her lead would say, 'Good girl, now we are going home,' and off she would go.

So, if you have a Yorkshire as a pet, teach it obedience, and tricks. It will mean giving time and exercising patience, but it will be a lot of fun for him and quite a bit for his owner, and to own a thoroughly well-trained pet instead of a pampered, spoiled little darling that takes no notice of any word of command is a great joy.

I have been asked so often by a prospective buyer: 'Shall I

have a dog or a bitch? Which would you say is best?' Well,
actually, there is not much to choose as regards temperament,
devotion and loyalty. As a companion, a bitch is thought to be
preferable by many, but some do not like to keep a bitch
because of the responsibility of having to keep her isolated for
about three weeks twice yearly. This is not such a trial now that
chemists have put on the market pills given by the mouth,
which take away the smell, thus discouraging the attentions of
the male dogs. There is also a lotion, which when applied to
the coat, will also help. A bitch is usually found to be more
personal in her attachment and an excellent house dog. I have
no preference, for a dog can be equally as affectionate and as
true as a bitch; it is just a matter of personal choice.

Travelling Holidays

Travelling with a Yorkshire Terrier can be a sheer delight, but
it can also be the most uncomfortable journey for all concerned. Going by road into the country, or to the seaside on
holiday, is no problem at all for men and women, it's just a
matter of changing headquarters. The pet, if he has been
trained, can also adjust himself and carries on just as if he were
in his own home. It is also evident that he gets a lot of enjoyment out of the changing scenery, the strange sounds and, of
course, the unusual smells, but if his human companions are
to derive the full pleasure of having their pet with them, preparations must be made as early as possible so that the dog is
properly trained for a long trip, and this, of course, involves an
obedience training. Wherever one is going to spend the night,
or if one is taking a holiday of a week or more, it is best when
applying for accommodation to ask whether one or more toy
dogs may accompany you. Sometimes the answer is definitely
'No', with a capital N, and may be underlined. Another
answers, 'Yes, so long as they are under control, but they cannot be allowed in the dining-room or recreation rooms',
which, of course, is quite right.

One answer we had was to the effect that big dogs were
allowed because they were well behaved, but on no account
could they allow toy dogs, because they went under the beds.
The obvious counter to this is that no matter what the breed or

size of the dog, it depends entirely on whether they have been trained or not.

I have travelled with my pets and show dogs all over the country, at one time taking three dogs and one bitch, and stayed at hotels. I have never had the awful anxiety of having to tidy up my room to leave it in order; indeed other residents, when I was putting the dogs in the car one day, remarked, 'Have you had them here all the time? We have never heard them.'

For satisfactory travelling it is absolutely necessary first for the dog to be thoroughly house-broken. Take him for exercise often and see that it is adequate. Exercise him immediately you are up in the morning, after feeding, and the last thing at night. While on the road stop at intervals for a little exercise and do not make the dog wait too long; generally he will try very hard to let you know his needs.

Secondly, get the dog accustomed to riding in the car before a long journey is to be taken. In the usual way, if a young puppy is held on the lap or up against the shoulders at first, he will soon get used to the motion of the car. Do this for a few minutes at first, gradually lengthen the spells, and hold him so that he can see out of the window. To put a dog on the floor, or below the level of the side of the car, is like a person staying in a cabin on a boat and not getting on deck into the fresh air. The result can be disastrous. Usually the dog gets so interested in the moving objects along the countryside that he becomes accustomed to the motion of the car and it does not bother him. A dog should not be taken for a car ride immediately after a meal.

Thirdly, it is absolutely essential to train the dog not to bark or whine even if left alone in a car or in a strange room, for there are others to be considered and to a tired traveller a noisy dog is disturbing to say the least.

Fourthly, try to train the dog to sit and stay; then windows can be left open, or even a door. It can be very annoying if a little dog suddenly runs up to you and, perhaps, catches a claw in your stockings, or a favourite frock. It must be remembered that not everyone likes dogs. Teach him to come when called. Teach him not to be destructive, not to scratch furniture or tear draperies or get on beds. If a cover is put on a chair then he can sit on it; also, where he is fed, a cover or even a newspaper on the floor will avoid leaving bits that may be trodden on. It is well to get a 'tiny' used to sleeping in a closed basket. He will be happy in his bed, and you will be at ease all night. If he *is* allowed to sleep on the bed, let him have his own blanket under him and when it is not in use, shake it out of doors, fold it neatly and put it away.

If a dog is well groomed there should be no fear of loose hair being left about; and be particular about cleaning his feet before he enters the room allotted to you, at all times. It is up to the owner to see that his dog is trained in such a way as to make a second visit to the same place a welcome one and it also helps to assure accommodation for other travellers.

Always when travelling take fresh water in, if possible, a thermos jug, to keep it cool. Some dogs when travelling will not eat or drink. It is a good plan to get the dog used to eating kinds of food different from what he is used to, in case it is not possible to follow his usual diet. A good tinned dog-food complete in itself is the easiest type of food, but do not forget a tin-opener!

Do not forget his lead, his brush and comb, his feeding dish, and the little blanket he is used to in his bed; also remember a favourite toy. This will not only be something for him to take to bed with him, but will relieve the tedium of the journey. Some dogs always suffer from travel sickness, but there are some good remedies on the market now or a veterinary surgeon will provide any one of several good prescriptions.

Most hotels will welcome a really well-behaved little pet. You will enjoy your stay, and he will be fascinated by the sea; or, if in the country, the various holes he will sniff at, made by wild life. If you have to leave him behind and he cannot stay in his own house try to get a friend that he knows to house him for the time; or a small boarding kennel where only the small type of dog is taken to stay. Although he will miss you, you will have the satisfaction of knowing he will be well cared for and that he will be safe. But always, if you possibly can, take him with you; he will be happier sharing your fun, and you will be happy, having his companionship.

11

Common Ailments and Nursing

Some well-known breeders always use homeopathic treatment for any disorders in their dogs, and contend that it is a much better method of cure for disordered health. The remedies which have curative properties will restore what is diseased without harm to what is healthy. They attack the disease and not the constitution of the dog.

It is always wise to have a thermometer, nail clippers, scissors, cotton wool, bandages, etc., handy. A thermometer is indispensable when treating a sick dog, for in most cases the temperature is the surest guide as to how the patient is progressing. It is a similar kind to that used by a doctor when he takes your temperature, though the normal temperature of a dog is higher than that of a human being. The best place to take a dog's temperature is in the rectum. The normal temperature is 101.5°F. and anything over that denotes fever. The point of the thermometer should be well covered with vaseline and inserted into the rectum for about two inches, where it should be left for about a minute, if a half-minute thermometer, which is best, is used. The dog must be held very firmly so that there is no risk of the thermometer breaking. The temperature can also be taken in the groin or the armpit, but it is necessary to leave the instrument, even a half-minute one, for two minutes. It must be well buried in the skin, otherwise a wrong temperature will result. The normal temperature in the armpit or the groin is a little lower than in the rectum and the method is not quite so easy nor so efficient. A special half-minute thermometer on which a dog's normal temperature is plainly marked is obtainable at most chemists. Always try to have help when taking a dog's temperature by holding him firmly so that he cannot wriggle.

Another important guide to a dog's health is the character and frequency of the pulse. The femoral artery is found on the inside of the dog's thigh, just as it crosses the thighbone. Place the fingers over the artery, and the beats felt per minute in health vary according to the size of the dog, but in the Yorkshire it is about ninety. When the pulse is very rapid, say one hundred and thirty, it is often a sign of fever, such as is found in distemper. A half-teaspoonful of brandy can be given, but do not delay in sending for a veterinary surgeon.

The condition of a dog is indicated by the gums and the tongue, which should be pink and clean; the eyes should be bright and clear. The nose should be damp and cool, but do not expect the nose to be perpetually cold, for when he is asleep he will often have a drier nose and not a very cold one. There is a difference, however, between a temporarily dry nose and the hot dry nose which stays that way even when the dog is running around; it may be the symptom of the starting of an illness.

General Administration of Medicine

If the medicine is to be given in the form of a powder, and there is not much taste to it, the best way to give it is to open the dog's mouth and shake it on to the back of the tongue. Close the mouth firmly and the dog will start to swallow. To open the mouth, take hold of the upper jaw with the left hand, with the tips of the fingers on the side and thumb on the other, gently press the cheeks betwen the teeth, when the dog will usually open his mouth. Raise the head backwards a little before the powder is dropped on the tongue. If there is any taste to the powder, try mixing it with food; a piece of meat divided up and the powder put in the middle is a good camouflage.

If a pill is to be given, open the mouth as already described and drop the pill as far as possible to the back of the mouth and then with the finger push it gently to the side of the mouth and gently down the throat. Close the mouth and hold it firmly until the dog has to swallow. If one releases the hold too quickly the pill is quite as quickly returned and one has to go through the performance all over again, the little dog not liking it at all. I have known a Yorkie hold a pill in the back of his throat for many seconds, and, thinking he had swallowed it, left him, only to find the pill on the floor.

However far down the finger may go, it will not make the dog retch. Be quite sure that the finger used is thoroughly cleansed and the nail cut short.

If fluid medicine is to be administered, a feeding spoon which prevents any of it being spilled is best; the patient thus getting the proper dose without its being spilled over his coat, making him uncomfortable and sticky. The best way to give it is to place one hand round the muzzle of the dog, so that his teeth are kept together, taking care not to press the tip of the nose which will cause him to gasp for breath. With the other hand, place the spout of the spoon just inside the lips. If an ordinary spoon is used, hold the muzzle in the same way, but with the finger and thumb of the other hand, make a pocket at the back of the mouth by pulling out the lower lip, and gently pour in. The dog will be forced to swallow it. A small bottle, with the exact amount of medicine in it, can be used in the same way, and if there is a sudden jerk of the dog's head, it will not spill as fluid in a spoon would do.

When nursing a sick dog everything required should be scrupulously clean. All the things required should be kept together in one place, or on a tray, and a bowl of water provided into which spoons that have been used for giving medicine or food can be dropped and washed at once and be ready for use again. After administration of medicine or food, gently wipe the dog's lips with a damp sponge or medicated gauze and dry gently with a very soft towel.

If a dog is very ill he requires more care and attention at night than during the day, for during the early hours the system is at its slowest and feeblest. Never give large quantities of nourishment at a time as it induces indigestion and often causes vomiting and diarrhoea, which of course are very weakening. Give little and often should be the rule. One or two teaspoonfuls is sufficient when given every two hours. As the dog regains strength more can be given, but gradually.

During illness the appetite is often so bad that it is difficult to know what to offer to encourage the patient to eat. He requires tempting, nourishing and easily digested food. Try not to force him to eat; a little food taken voluntarily does much more good. A good idea is to get a piece of liver, or something that the patient especially likes, dip it into the milk food or meat juices and he will often lick it off, but do not let him get the piece of liver. To obtain the meat juice get a piece of raw, lean, juicy steak, and press as much of the liquid out as possible, or scrape it with a spoon when the meat will be as soft and smooth as jelly, or use one of the Brand's essences. An excellent food can be made from a small quantity of beef, mutton and veal. Cut the meat into small pieces, one pound to a pint of water, and slowly simmer (do not boil) for about three hours, strain, and when cold it will be a thick jelly. Give it warm, with a little brown bread crumbs. In the jelly form, if a little is put on the lips, the dog will lick it into his mouth. The giblets of a chicken can be cooked in the same manner and given as a jelly.

Most dogs are fond of rabbit, which is, of course, very nourishing. It can be given as a change, and treated in the same way as the meat. Sheep's kidney grilled and mixed with a few brown bread crumbs is also good. All kinds of fish can be given, boiled or even fried, but they must be not too fatty; a fried herring is the most nourishing. Sheep's brains are very well liked and should be cooked in a little milk until very tender. As the invalid improves, all sorts of tasty meals can be made to encourage the appetite to become normal.

Robinson's infant cereal makes a good liquid food for a dog on a light diet, and contains no egg, which could be better for some. If this is poured over a sponge cake, the type used for making a trifle, it makes a nutritious meal and is easily digested. This is also very good for puppy-rearing.

The vitality of the tiny Yorkshire Terrier is amazing and normally, with care and attention, he will soon be on his feet again after a most distressing illness and be as cheeky as ever before. Oh, how spoilt he can be when ill! He has probably slept in his owner's room and possibly, if very ill, taken right into bed. The little fellow does not forget all the extra fuss and his look of disappointment when made to return to his own bed may well tempt the indulgent owner to say, 'All right, but only for tonight.' Unless you want a permanent companion to sleep with, you must be strict and not give way even for one night. Bad habits are not easily broken.

A coat in winter is absolutely unnecessary unless, of course, the dog has been ill, when it is very foolish *not* to give him the extra warmth. A good idea for a coat is to take an old, thick woollen sock, cut off the foot and cut two holes a few inches apart for the back legs to go through, and two for the front legs. The part that goes round the neck should be the ribbed part of the sock and this can be turned back forming a collar which will make it very cosy. If one wishes and has a few minutes to spare, a stitching can be made around the cut parts. This will stop fraying and, if it is done in a bright wool, gives it a decorative effect. For the young puppy a child's woolly sock done in the same way is ideal and very easy to put on; no ties are necessary and it makes a cosy fitting, close to the body. When the dog is getting better, pieces of the coat can be cut off from time to time so that the sudden loss of extra warmth is not noticed.

If a dog is suffering from constipation, a teaspoonful of medicated paraffin given daily, until the condition has improved, is excellent; indeed, a weekly dose is quite good for all dogs. The paraffin, being only a lubricant, does not purge.

If a dog is listless and has a dry nose and refuses food, take his temperature and if it is above normal send for your veterinary surgeon. Sometimes this condition will last only for a day, but in any case have him looked over; it is often the start of a bad chill or even distemper, and if attention is given at the early stage there is every chance of a speedy recovery. If left, serious complications may occur. Keep him very warm and quiet, and do not persist in trying to make him take food; for the time being he is better without, at least until the O.K. has been given by the veterinary surgeon.

The Anal Glands

I mentioned the anal glands in a previous chapter. Congestion of these glands can be very troublesome. The dog so affected will draw himself into a sitting position and then drag himself

along the ground. Often this action has been mistaken for the
dog having worms. The secretion or fluid escaping from these
glands, as it often will when the glands are congested, gives off
an obnoxious odour, as if the dog has passed wind. This is
most unpleasant when a dog lives in the house. Apply a hot
fomentation, a piece of flannel wrung out in very hot water will
do. Place it on the gland and very gently squeeze with the
finger and thumb; this will release the matter accumulated in
the gland. Sometimes it is necessary to attend to these glands
frequently. If the glands are sore apply a little boracic, or zinc
and castor-oil ointment.

If persistent diarrhoea has caused prolapsus of the lower
bowel, or rectum, which has become inflamed and swollen,
take hold of the dog by the hind legs and with a thoroughly
clean and well-vaselined finger apply firm pressure, when the
extrusion will slip back into place. Until the trouble has
abated, starchy foods will be best, for a time at least.

If the trouble recurs the same treatment will be necessary,
but in persistent cases a veterinary surgeon must be
consulted.

Balanitis

This is a mattery discharge which flows from the prepuce in
drops. There is always a certain amount of discharge from the
prepuce, but in health the dog keeps himself clean. Syringe
with solution of one part T.C.P. and five parts water and the
condition will usually improve. Always be careful to see that
after a mating the sheath is well over the prepuce and that no
hairs have been left inside as this will cause inflammation
and irritation.

Catarrh

A cold in the head can make a little dog very miserable; he
sneezes and coughs and a watery discharge comes from the
eyes and nose. After a few days the nasal discharge becomes a
thick mucous, making the breathing very laboured. To
relieve, give an inhalation of friars balsam. Cover the head

Int. Ch. Mr Pimm of
Johnstounburn

A 'Yorkie' with his coat tied up

Six Johnstounburn Champions
Pimbrom, Mr Pimm, Myrtle, Tufty, Medium, Pipit

Ch. Robina Gay of Yadnum

Ch. Blairsville Royal Seal

Ch. Yadnum Regal Fare (*Sally Anne Thompson*)

Ch. Polliam Sweet Delight

Ch. Candytops Royal Cascade

Ch. Candytops Strawberry Fare (*C. M. Cooke*)

with a towel, in the same way as for a human, but do not make
the solution so strong, and do not leave the little patient under
long enough for the fumes to get into the eyes. They can be
covered with a little cotton wool or a bandage. Keep the eyes
well cleaned; bathe with Optrex and put in a little Golden Eye
Ointment to relieve the soreness. There is no fever with
catarrh and so it is easily distinguishable from distemper or
hard pad, when the temperature will rise to 103°F. or more.

Constipation

The motion of a healthy dog should be firm, not too stiff, and
of brown colour. If the liver is disordered the stool will be a
light sandy shade and hard. Many pets suffer from constipation and it is more often than not the result of unsuitable feeding and no proper exercise. Sometimes the dog will cry out
when attempting to relieve himself and after a struggle will be
left very sore. Do not allow this condition to continue as it may
result in an obstruction or stoppage of the bowels. Give a daily
dose of medicated paraffin; a teaspoonful to a puppy and a
dessertspoonful to an adult. This is very safe as the paraffin is
not a purgative, but acts as a lubricant. If a larger amount than
is actually necessary is given it will do no harm whatsoever.

A little Milk of Magnesia given in a little milk will help.

Convulsions

These usually occur in puppies, but of course an adult can
have them. In a puppy a convulsion or fit is sometimes
brought about by the presence of worms or often during the
changing of the puppy teeth to the permanent ones. If a puppy
is dosed with a reliable worm medicine at an early age, say six
weeks, or on leaving the mother, worm fits should not then
occur. A convulsion is not a disease; it is a symptom of disorder. The puppy should be placed in a warm darkened
room, away from any other dogs. If the convulsion is bad a
small piece of wood or a wad of material should be placed be-

tween the jaws to prevent him biting his tongue. A cool damp
cloth applied to the skull will help. Tablets are available for
this condition, but it is better to consult your veterinary surgeon to find out the cause, especially if the fits persist.

Diarrhoea

Your dog can have a loose motion without having diarrhoea
but the complaint itself is a most distressing and weakening
condition. Should he pass a watery-like motion with a horrible
smell, this is usually diarrhoea. Unsuitable food or a change of
living conditions can sometimes be the cause, but it is usually
a bacterial infection. Some low-grade bacterial infections,
although not too serious will need veterinary attention and
anything more severe most certainly will. If your dog has a
loose motion, first aid treatment can be given. Kaopectate,
which you can purchase from your main chemist shop, is very
good. The dosage for an adult dog will be a small teaspoonful
three times a day; for a puppy smaller quantities. If there is any
temperature rise or any trace of blood, do not delay and get
the veterinary surgeon immediately. If neglected this condition will prove fatal, but modern drugs can prevent this.
During the time your dog is ill, restrict him from drinking
large quantities of water, but small amounts of warm water
will prevent him becoming dehydrated. Take him off all food
for 24 hours, then no red meat, milk, biscuit meal or the like.
Give him small amounts of steamed fish or chicken and
diluted milk and water for a few days, or a moistened sponge
cake, then ease him back into his usual diet by degrees.

Distemper

This is a disease solely the result of infection and it is *not*
necessary for all dogs to have it. To a puppy under three
months old it is usually fatal. Distemper cannot be cured by
any known medicine but a dog can be made immune by
inoculation. Dogs not suffering from the disease can be
carriers of the germs and infect others. Extra care must be
taken; disinfect a dog who has been to a show, *before* he mixes

with the other inmates of the kennel. The first symptoms of the disease are that the dog becomes dull and languid, has an indifferent appetite and, if food is taken, it is vomited. Sometimes diarrhoea accompanies these symptoms and the dog is feverish, the temperature often rising to 104°F. It may drop and be nearly normal and then rise again. The teeth become covered with a yellow fur, leaving them discoloured with brown spots, and if this condition stays it is called distemper teeth. In a young patient mattery spots may appear on the belly. The eyes are dull and watery. The nose in the early stages may be moist but soon becomes dry. If the lungs are affected a watery discharge tinged with blood will come from the nose. The patient will lose flesh very rapidly. Keep the dog as warm as possible, by artificial heat in winter, and on a very light diet. Feed a cold and starve a fever is a very true saying. Send for a veterinary surgeon.

The Ear

Ear troubles are a nuisance which cause the dog very much discomfort, in some cases pain, and they can be most unpleasant for his owner. A short description of the most common conditions will I hope be useful. The most frequent ear disease in the dog is caused by mites, by fungus infections, or by bacterial infection, and sometimes by a combination of all these. With the presence of tiny mites in the ear the disease is known as parasitic canker and when seen through an instrument, the ear-canal is inflamed and there is a dark-brown waxy substance. The mites themselves cannot be seen with the naked eye. Although the brown deposit may be seen externally, the ear itself is quite dry, with no sign of fluid discharge whatsoever.

When the dog holds his head on one side, and constantly shakes it or continuously scratches the ear, the cause may be that wax has accumulated. A very good oil, Bob Martin's Canker Lotion, can be applied. Drop a little of the oil right into the ear and work it around the base. Or, on to a matchstick which has been lighted and the black end rubbed off, roll tightly round it a little cotton wool and wet with the oil. Insert this into the ear and very, very gently work into the base, but do not delve too deeply as the ear is a very delicate feature and easily injured. Change the cotton wool on the match-stick until it comes out of the ear clean. It is astonishing how much brown wax can be extracted. There are many preparations on the market for ear infections. Otodex Veterinary Ear Drops, a liquid which is easily squirted into the ear, seems to bring a dark wax-like substance to the surface. This can easily be wiped away with cotton wool. If there is a horrible smell from the ear the dog may have canker. In some cases you can treat this yourself, but in severe cases your vet will prescribe a stronger type of medication.

Excessive cleaning of the ear channel should be avoided. The ear channel is very long and because the lower part is curved it is impossible to clean it by ordinary means.

Bacterial and fungus infections are responsible for the more serious discharging condition which often becomes chronic. In a condition like this the discharge is the outstanding feature, and may be seen on the outside of the ear, or may be detected by the squelching sound that is made if a slight massage is given at the base of the dog's ear. The very unpleasant smell is also an indication. If seen through an auroscope, or tiny ear instrument, at the end of which is a bright light, the ear-canal can be seen to be intensely inflamed and red, also the accumulation of discharge and sometimes blood mixed with it. It is of no use trying to clean the ears by just ramming down cotton wool; one must have great patience and gently clean the ear with any of the preparations I have mentioned.

Just how dogs' ears become infected is not always easy to decide, but I have heard of a Yorkshire who was perfectly free of any ear trouble when he went to his new home, becoming affected after a short time. The cause was traced to the household cat; so it is contagious. Drop-eared dogs must pick up dirt and germs, and certain types of ears are prone to unhealthy conditions. An abrasion of the ear channel may provide a port of entry, and this is particularly likely to occur where the parasitic condition already exists.

Any foreign body in the ear is a frequent source of infection and during the summer the forerunner is the notorious grass seed, which has been known to puncture the ear drum. The actual removal from the ear may cause unavoidable cuts and when extracted an antiseptic application could be applied. Treatment of these ear infections is difficult and often unsatisfactory, and it is far better to seek the advice of a veterinary surgeon.

Many preparations have been used in the treatment of discharging ears, and very good results have been obtained by the application of ointments containing penicillin, streptomycin and terramycin. In some cases silver preparations are effective in the treatment of fungus.

Another ailment has the name of haematoma. It is a swelling inside the ear-flap like a small balloon, which forms through the ear-flap having had a bang. It is really a large blood blister and is not painful to the dog when touched. Some think that the best way to cure it is to open the blister and let the watery contents escape; others say leave well alone, but however it is treated, more often than not it produces a deformity of the ear-flap due to the inside skin contracting, leaving the dog with what is called a boxer's, or cauliflower, ear.

Eclampsia

The nursing bitch is always susceptible to this complaint. During the gestation period the puppies are taking a great deal of the bitch's calcium, and she still continues to lose it all the time the puppies are dependent on her for food.

A bitch will seem to be quite fit while feeding her family, when suddenly, without any warning, she will collapse, being unable to raise herself or walk, though at the same time she is quite conscious. A veterinary surgeon must be called and by an injection of calcium boro-gluconate a cure is invariably effected. If neglected the symptoms become worse and the patient has little chance of recovering. A liberal supply of calcium and vitamin D before and during pregnancy and when suckling, should be given.

The Eye

Seldom does a Yorkshire Terrier suffer from ingrowing eyelashes, but with the Pekingese the percentage is fairly large. When the lashes are ingrowing they touch the eye and cause ulcers, which are very painful and can be very damaging to the eye. To improve the condition smear a little Golden Eye Ointment on the eyelids and gently fold upwards. In all such cases try to consult a veterinary surgeon

If a dog's eye gets scratched by another dog or by a thorn in the garden, or even by his own claw, bathe with a good boracic eye lotion or Optrex and put in Golden Eye Ointment.

In inflammation of the eye, the pupil is cloudy and the white of the eye red and there is an intolerance to light and a discharge of tears or, in a bad case, a mattery discharge. Sometimes a film forms and covers the eye completely; this is called a blue eye. Soak a piece of lint with the eye lotion and after placing some Golden Eye Ointment in the eye cover with the lint and a bandage. Also bandage the foot on the side of the affected eye so as to prevent the dog rubbing it. Try to prevent the dog from rubbing the eye and keep him in a darkened room for a few days. If a dog just suffers from a slight weakness of the eyes apply a little Golden Eye Ointment on retiring.

Gastritis

A dog with this complaint quickly loses weight and his condition generally deteriorates. The dog will vomit food and liquid. Take him off all food and milk. Do not let him drink large amounts of water, but small amounts of warm water will help prevent him becoming dehydrated. Mild attacks can be helped by doses of Kaopectate, but if there is an increase in his temperature or signs of blood in the vomit, do not delay and contact your veterinary surgeon. Gastritis can be accompanied by diarrhoea and could be gastro enteritis. This must be treated by a vet, as an antibiotic injection is the only thing that will help. Modern drugs are so improved that the loss of a dog with this complaint is unusual these days.

Hard-pad

This is also called para-distemper. It was thought by some to have been brought into England during the war by the pets of soldiers. It is today's canine scourge, and is much more serious than distemper, because it usually shows no definite symptoms. Tackled at once and with careful nursing it is really much less frightening. Years ago the huge death roll from distemper was, as any veterinary surgeon will maintain, lack of observation of the less-skilled dog owners in suspecting the disease, thus treatment was delayed and the result often fatal. Hard-pad is much more difficult to detect because, beyond a rise in temperature, there are, at first, no other symptoms. Some of the distemper symptoms may appear followed by a nervous disorder, the dog being listless and shunning the light. Hardness of the pad may develop. The temperature rises to around 103°F., inflammation of the brain often being the cause. When this happens it is very serious for the poor dog and in some cases he has to be destroyed. Veterinary surgeons have in the past been baffled by the disease, but a new and non-virulent vaccine has been discovered, which claims to immunize a dog against hard-pad and distemper. Immunization is not effective until the puppy is three months old. Some veterinary surgeons will give what they call a preliminary shot, but that lasts only a week or two.

Hernia

This is a protrusion of a part of the tummy. If at the navel it is called umbilical hernia. So long as it remains small and soft it is usually regarded as not being harmful and, with time, will often disappear. Inguinal hernia is a swelling in the groin and if a bitch is suffering from this condition she should not be bred from. An operation can be performed to put matters right.

Kennel Cough

A virus which is transmitted from an infected dog anywhere.

Places you are most likely to pick it up are, for instance, parks or exercise areas, your vet's waiting room, training classes and even boarding kennels, although most kennels insist that your dog is inoculated against it. The inoculation is given nasally. The cough is rough and harsh and can cause the dog much distress. A dose of Benylin, child's strength, can help to soothe but your vet can give an antibiotic which will help to clear it up. Watch out for signs of recurrence.

Offensive Breath

A disordered stomach is sometimes the cause of offensive breath, or it may be due to worms. It can also be caused by the accumulation of tartar on the teeth. If the presence of worms is suspected give a tried worm medicine. If it is the teeth, and they are not too bad with tartar, get a piece of very thin old linen, wet it, and with the finger, dip it into a little bicarbonate of soda, very gently rubbing it around the teeth. This will help to loosen the tartar and with a tooth scraper you may be able to scale the tartar off. It is a job not liked by any dog and great care must be taken not to injure the gums; they quickly bleed, and a very sore mouth will be the result. Do not be alarmed if the dog swallows any of the powder; it is quite harmless and, in fact, is good for the digestion. Another cleanser is a little peroxide applied in the same way as bicarbonate of soda. It is seldom that a dog who is allowed bones to chew gets tartar. If the stomach is disordered, a daily dose of Milk of Magnesia will relieve the condition.

Parasites

Most dogs, even the well-kept, well-groomed Yorkshire Terriers will sometimes house a few unwelcome guests.

Fleas To the long-coated dog these insects are very troublesome, the irritation and the scratching often inducing eczema, so it is for this reason that the pests must be promptly destroyed. A wash in an insecticidal shampoo, and there are many on the market, will kill any live pests on the dog and will remove some of the eggs. Further washes will be necessary. The dog's bedding and anywhere he is likely to rest must be sprayed with a suitable spray or dusted with insect powder. Here again there are several on the market but stubborn visitors may need extra strong repellants which you can get from your vet.

Harvest Bugs   These microscopic red insects look like grains of red sand, which, as their name implies, appear at harvest time. They cause a lot of irritation, the dog scratching and licking the affected parts. The parts affected are around the nose, the bend of the elbows, just in the front of the hocks, and on the stomach. If treated in the same way as for fleas they are easily and quickly got rid of.

Lice   This insect is smaller than a flea, and is bluey-grey in colour, adhering to the dog's skin by the proboscis, making the insects look as if they are standing on their heads. These can be got rid of if treated in like manner as the flea.

Ticks   A field where sheep graze can be absolutely infested with these very irritating insects. They are bluish-grey in colour and vary in size, some being as large as a pea or small bean. The usual places to find them are on the head, ears and neck, but they can be found on any part of the body. They fix themselves firmly to the skin of the dog with suckers and the only way to remove them is to pick them off with a pair of forceps. Your vet will prescribe a suitable remedy if the products you can buy from your pet shop do not work.

Mange   This is a parasitic disease contagious to dogs and people. The parts affected are around the eyes, outside the flaps of the ears, the elbows, the hocks and the tummy, but it gradually spreads all over the body if not taken in hand very quickly. The parts become bare and are covered with red spots and the skin becomes covered with sores and scales, which are caused by incessant scratching. If treated properly it can be cured in a very short time.

This condition can only successfully be diagnosed by your vet who will prescribe the correct treatment. Modern drugs make such treatment quicker and more effective than remedies from the past, many of which are no longer on the market.

Follicular Mange   This is a very loathsome disease, and is usually confined to puppies and young dogs. Adult dogs seldom catch it. Its progress is gradual; the puppy may at first have a few bare round spots, the skin looking greyish or dirty. There is much irritation. If not checked, the bare places increase in size and, later, dark red or blue pimples form which, when squeezed, exude matter, a dark blood-coloured fluid. It is in this matter that the parasite is found. When one of these mattery spots is broken, the parasite, and the eggs, get on to another part of the dog's body. They can be seen only under a microscope and look rather like worms. The hair continues to fall out and the skin gets thicker. Dogs in good health have white skin. When affected by this disease the skin assumes a dirty-greyish colour and is covered with thick scales.

This condition can only be correctly diagnosed by a vet, who will prescribe the proper treatment.

Ringworm This complaint is caused through a vegetable parasite and is very contagious to other dogs, and to human beings. It appears at first as a small bare patch on the skin and perfectly round, hence its name. The fungus is on the outside of the ring and as it works it makes the hair in that area fall out. The attack can be on any part of the body, and the skin affected is generally slightly rough and sometimes has small red patches on it. For treatment consult a veterinary surgeon.

Always when in doubt consult your veterinary surgeon. A little knowledge is sometimes dangerous and it is the duty of every owner or breeder of a dog to do the best possible to relieve the patient.

Parvovirus

When this was first diagnosed in the late seventies, there was no recognized inoculation which would give any immunity. Canine Parvovirus is closely related to a virus which causes enteritis in cats and so cat inoculation was used. Now an inoculation is available which gives a certain amount of immunity. Puppies lose the immunity they have from their mothers when they are weaned and so early inoculation is advisable, although this has in some cases caused the death of a puppy. The symptoms are acute diarrhoea and sickness, the dog is obviously very ill and you must get it to the vet as soon as possible. Dehydration occurs very rapidly and even when a drip has been set up the dog may not survive. In the case of puppies and old dogs their chances of survival are small and death can occur within the space of a few hours.

Rheumatism

This complaint can occur in dogs of all ages, is due mostly to chills or damp, and seems to occur in any part of the body. The muscles at the back of the neck are a very vulnerable point, the dog being unable to put his head down except with difficulty. When the loins are affected the dog walks stiffly and with an arched back, and will often cry out when touched. He will sometimes lose the use of his hind legs, and when he moves the joints can be heard to crack. A good liniment rubbed into the affected part will take the stiffness out of the muscle. If a dog gets very wet while exercising take care to dry him thoroughly, especially his tummy and legs, and never let a dog who is still damp lie around.

Rickets

This affects puppies who are not fed properly, or their mother did not get the proper food during gestation. Although they may be in a well-ventilated warm room, and are not allowed their freedom this may bring it on. There is no doubt that confinement is one of the principal causes of this complaint, but worms are often the cause. The symptoms are swollen joints, especially the knees and hocks. The front legs become bowed and the ankles weak, and the puppy walks on the back of his legs instead of his feet, hence the term 'down on his pasterns'. The back legs are bent and the hock turned inwards, the term 'cow hocked' meaning this condition. A puppy should be given a chemical food and when given regularly for some considerable time it will help effect a cure. Cod-liver oil, halibut oil or Shaw's Everfree can be given, also a calcium tablet daily, and plenty of rich-in-iron nourishing food. Perhaps the puppy is in a new home and if there are children, naturally excited at their new addition to the family, he is often kept on the go. He is played with and pulled around, in fact he is given a lively time by these little ones, and a short nap now and again is all he gets. Make him rest for longer periods during the day and he will soon get stronger limbs. A little lime-water added to his drinking-water is splendid for strengthening the bones.

Stings

A dog in play will often snap at an insect, resulting in the dog being stung on the lip or in the mouth. If you can see the sting remove it quickly, either with your finger nails or tweezers. If you already know your dog is allergic to stings he must have an injection to prevent too much swelling. Antihistimine cream can be applied to an outside sting, but on the lip or tongue can be dangerous and your vet can give him an injection. Try to train your dog not to chase and catch insects. Stings can be nasty.

Toes

Always see that the nails are fairly short, for during exercise a long one can get broken and cause a great deal of pain. If a nail is broken right up in the fleshy part of the toe, bathe with boracic powder added to warm water. The dog will lick and lick (Nature's way of healing), but if it does not respond to this treatment, tie the foot up for a time, bathing it each day to keep the wound free from dirt. A cyst is a swelling between the toes. It has an inflamed appearance and is most painful, making the dog limp, or unable to put the foot to the ground. Bathe in very warm boracic water and with the continual licking of the dog it will soon become soft and will quickly break. A poultice will hasten the time for the swelling to break.

Travel Sickness

(*see* page 106)

12

For the Novice

It is better to buy a puppy, or an adult dog, direct from a breeder who has a reputation to uphold. There will be many more puppies to be seen from which a selection can be made. The breeder will be interested and pleased to hear about the puppy's progress and will gladly give sound advice in the management and correct feeding of the puppy. Usually he will supply a diet sheet so that the dog continues to have the same kind and amount of food as he has been used to.

Ask the breeder as many questions as you can think of regarding the many little things that have to be done for the puppy. Has he been wormed? Has he been inoculated? Is he house clean; if not, about how long will it take? All such questions are readily answered by the breeder, who is only too pleased to help because it is for the comfort and welfare of the puppy after he has left his care.

Who is the nearest breeder to my home, or who would it be best to get a puppy from, is quite easy to answer. Ring up the Kennel Club and you will be put in touch with reliable breeders.

If the puppy is under three months of age he may have received preliminary inoculations. Some breeders like to use these as a precaution but the effect is shortlived and further inoculations will be necessary. When the puppy is twelve weeks old he will need to be inoculated against distemper, hard pad, parvovirus, hepatitis and leptospirosis. This may be given in two or three parts, with a two-week interval between each shot. I prefer three parts, the parvovirus shot being the last of the three and so given as a separate inoculation. During the period of four or six weeks the puppy should not be taken to any place visited by other dogs such as parks or commons and should not be taken to any public place for two weeks following the last inoculation. Great progress has been made over the past years in making these inoculations more effective and the preventive power, although not one hundred percent, means the puppy will have good protection should he come up against these ailments.

The Yorkshire, in this country, is traditionally the working-man's breed, and quite a high proportion of past and present champions have been bred in small kennels, where the care of the dogs has to be undertaken in the evenings and at weekends.

The breed is not an expensive one to run if care is taken over the essentials, but loving care means far more than anything else. An enthusiast will travel weary journeys by rail or road to dog shows, taking his dog in his travelling case, all the equip-ment for grooming, a little refreshment for master and dog in another case, all in the hope that the dog may be a lucky win-ner. If not, plans are made on the return journey for the next time. It can be great fun, and what a delightful crowd of people exhibitors can be!

Shyness

The owner of a shy dog can do quite a lot to minimize this most unfortunate condition by giving the dog a somewhat dif-ferent treatment. He need not, in any way, be spoilt, but he can be given special consideration over things that cause him to be nervous. Say, for instance, that he is scared when a vacuum cleaner is being used. The carpets must be cleaned, so why not let him into the garden or put him in another room while this is being done? Sometimes the noisy play of children will shatter him; if so, keep him quietly with you while it is going on. It must be remembered, if he is so shy, he is not quite mentally up to standard, but a spell of treatment for the nerves will, in most cases, put him right. Benerva tablets are good. Although some will always be upset at noises, others, even during a thunderstorm, will take no notice, while others will hide in the most awkward places, but as soon as the noises cease will come out and be quite normal. This reminds me of an incident that happened many years ago. We had been out visiting and it was one of the rare occasions when the dog had to be left at home. We were not away long, but during that time there was a thunderstorm, and when we returned, to our horror, the room where we had left the dog was empty. We couldn't think where she could be until we heard a slight noise by the fireplace, on investigating we found our dog, rather darker than usual, up the chimney. It was one of the old-fashioned kind with a register that shut down. In her fright she had gone up the chimney and the register had fallen down blocking her exit. It was a nasty moment for us, but we made sure that it would not happen again.

Conditioning the Coat

If the general health of the Yorkshire Terrier is impaired the fact is registered in his skin and hair, which loses that natural softness, elasticity, smoothness and lustre. As the complexion of a human is cleaned and brightened by exercise, so is the dog's skin and coat improved by the same means.

While hygienic and dietetic influences act upon man and dog in the same way outwardly the salutary effect is much less quickly seen in the dog. He may have been ill and long since recovered, and yet his coat will still be dry and staring, but if the dog is in good health, this same condition may exist through lack of grooming.

Even if a dog is well and has been faithfully cared for there is always work to be done on this coat before he can be shown at his best. The amount and character of the work to be put in on the coat depends upon conditions. If the dog is kept right— that is, properly fed, given ample exercise and groomed regularly— his coat should always be in a fair condition and the work of bringing it to its best should be comparatively easy. If the fine, smooth and glossy texture is missing, however, and the coat is coarse and staring, then several months may be required to get it into condition.

If the skin is still dry after well grooming, use olive oil or coconut oil liberally all over the body for a few days. Try to keep a very thin coat on the dog, otherwise he will, in all probability, rub the oil off either on his bed or on the furniture. After washing the oil out, it would be well for the dog to wear a jacket for a short time. One does not usually put a jacket on a Yorkshire Terrier, but it would be advisable when the hair is very rough and staring. It will keep the hair down, a moderate degree of heat being conducive to fine hair, and the extra warmth tends to make the coat fine and glossy.

Groom once a day to get the coat in prime condition and if this is continued for several weeks, plus proper diet and sufficient exercise, he should be in ideal condition and ready to be shown. Oil given inwardly is beneficial for the conditioning of the coat. For those who always have their dog around them, this is a better method than greasing the actual coat, for one does not always want an apron on.

It has been recorded that the weavers in Scotland and the North of England used to have their pets with them while at work and great competition went on between them as to whose dog had the longest coat. The pets were Clydesdale and Skye Terriers. In the process of making the cloth lanoline was used, and when the weaver's hands became too oily they wiped them on their dogs. It was thought that this improved the growth of the coat. Lanoline is still used today by some to promote the growth of the hair.

Doubtless some who contemplate showing will say that it is utterly impossible for them to devote too much time to their dog, but if they wish to succeed they will find that it is essential.

A very good conditioner for the coat is to wash the dog, not with soap, but with egg. This method can be used occasionally but it cannot be held superior to a good-quality soap. However, for those who would care to give an egg shampoo, here are the directions. Break two eggs in a basin and beat sufficiently to mix the white with the yolks. Wet the coat with warm water and thoroughly work the eggs into a lather, rubbing well into the skin. After the dog has been well massaged have someone ready to pour water over him while you continue to massage until every trace of the egg has been washed out of the coat. Any trace of eggs will leave the coat sticky. If it is at all possible wash the dog in rainwater; its natural softness gives lustre to the coat.

If the coat is very straggly and thin at the base, cut an inch or two off all round; this will strengthen the coat and make him look much tidier.

People and dogs alike, the growth of hair differs on individuals. Some women have exceedingly long hair while with others it just grows to shoulder length and stops, and no matter what treatment it receives, nothing will improve the length, although the condition may be good, and it may be bright and shiny. So it is with some dogs; but the fact remains, a daily grooming does keep the coat in condition, but it is no use doing it well one day and then forgetting all about it until such time as it is all entangled. A little brushing is far better than none.

Business

No special business ability is needed if dogs are to be kept purely as a hobby, but when the task of breeding and selling is undertaken, this is a serious matter. It can, to a certain extent, be a profitable business, though to try to make a livelihood out of it would be a risky chance. Some look on breeding purely as a hobby with no thought of profit, and will sell their stock very cheaply, or give an occasional puppy to a relative or friend. The gift puppy is not a good policy, for people seldom value such a gift as much as they would had they paid just a small amount. A pure-bred, healthy, carefully reared puppy is valuable; a small charge to help the breeder cover rearing costs, and the buyer will appreciate the puppy more and take more care of it.

There are others whose only thought is to produce puppies for commercial gain. So long as each puppy is turned into cash as soon as it can leave its mother, they do not care whether the buyer is satisfied. It is a wise plan for beginners, for the first few years, to sell all the puppies from each litter, except perhaps one that it is thought will make a brood. If, when she is mature, she has not fulfilled the promise she gave, it is best to sell her as soon as possible, for it is essential to keep the numbers down in a kennel if it is to pay.

The money received from the sale of a litter ought to cover the costs incurred in the production and rearing of the puppies and perhaps show a small profit. The stud fee will vary and will be governed by the bloodlines in the stud dog's pedigree, the extent of his championship wins and the quality of his progeny, the extra food for the dam, the costs of extra heating, lighting and cooking, which often come out of the general household expenses, all add up and should be taken

into account. Out of an average litter of Yorkshire Terriers,
two may be larger than the others and they can be sold at
about £65 to £70, the other smaller ones for perhaps a little
more. Offer the puppies at various prices, graduating the price
according to the promise of the puppy. A pet will not command the same price as one that is outstanding and will make
a show dog. If a breeder is not known—by that I mean if his
stock is not known—he cannot expect to get the same prices as
a well-known breeder. It is much better to sell the puppies at a
fair price than to hang on to them hoping for a better price. It
costs money to keep a puppy and the price obtained when the
puppy is six months old or more will not be in proportion to
the cost of his keep, therefore the profit is less. The older a dog
gets the harder it is to place him, unless he is a really outstanding, beautiful specimen and it is hoped will make an excellent
stud. It is usually difficult to place puppies when they are between the age of five and nine months. For the novice,
therefore, it is a better plan, until he gains experience and a
reputation for breeding good stock, to sell the puppies while
they are still young.

It may take many years to build up a reputation, so fair dealing and the breeding of good stock is essential. There are two
factors contributing to the reputation of a kennel: the first is
showing successfully, and the second, advertising. The first
dog to be exhibited is usually one that has been bought, but as
the exhibitor gains experience, a home-bred is proudly shown
and if it wins at a few shows, a start has been made for further
successes. For a kennel to go ahead financially, showing must
be frequent, for unless seen around the shows one is soon
forgotten. It is continually necessary to advertise stock for sale.
The best mediums are the weekly canine papers, but a small
advertisement in a local paper will often be the means of selling a puppy as a pet. The best way to advertise is to give the
true facts of the stock for sale, not to praise the virtues too
much or omit the faults. A disillusioned buyer is no recommendation for further sales. Recommendations are the means
of future sales, and the good reputation of a kennel is one of
the highest points to aim for. Remember that a puppy can
change very much in his first few months of growing up, so try
not to think of all the geese as swans.

It is a very dangerous practice to send a puppy, or in fact any dog, on approval, for if a puppy is returned, he may have been in contact with an infection and this will be brought into your kennel. If the journey has been a long one, the horrors of travelling any distance in a basket or crate will take a long time to overcome, and he may suffer from nervousness as a result of this. To him, big changes are occurring in his young life. I know it is not always possible for a prospective buyer to visit the kennel, but if a true picture of the puppy is painted, his faults as well as his good points included, and the price is reasonable for what he really is, then the buyer will be satisfied.

Buyers from overseas trust the breeders of repute and count on getting value for their money. To betray this trust and tradition by sending out a puppy or an adult dog that does not come up to the standard, or that has been wrongly described, or priced exorbitantly not only injures the breeder's reputation but British Dogdom in general.

When a sale is made from the recommendation of another breeder, it is usual for the seller to pay a commission of ten per cent of the purchase price, whatever it is, large or small, to the recommender. An advertisement may have appeared in a paper, but the prospective buyer may not have seen the advertisement and may have been recommended by another breeder, so it is always best to ask from what source he learned that you had puppies for sale. If a sale is effected and the enquiry came from another breeder it is only fair and business-like to give commission, then further enquiries will be passed on.

All these remarks have been offered for the benefit of breeders just starting, those who love the Yorkshire Terrier and want to make rearing him a success. The Yorkie is the most popular toy breed in registrations at the Kennel Club, with a good percentage of exports. My advice to the novice is, be fair in all your dealings with clients and at the same time be fair to yourself, then you will succeed.

In running a kennel of show dogs, or for pets, there are many things to think of and one is apt to lose sight of them. Never put off a job thinking that it can be done another time, for in these very busy times they just don't get done. Always keep in mind that livestock of any kind, especially tiny dogs, cannot take care of themselves. If they are forgotten or neglected in any way, they are liable to suffer both in body and mind. A dog can be very happy or very bored, he can be comfortable or the reverse, so he must be made as happy and contented as possible and it is up to you, the owner, to see that this is done. One need not be a salve to work, although where several dogs are kept there is always enough to do; nevertheless with a thought-out plan of routine, you will be able to do all jobs quickly and efficiently and the time saved can be spent on other jobs not connected with dogs. Do not become a slave to your dogs.

Nursing a sick dog is one of the times when a lot of patience is needed. A good nurse is a treasure to a doctor and a sympathetic nurse to a tiny dog is a godsend. Some women, and some men, have a flair for nursing and, by their common sense, seem to know exactly how the patient is feeling, sensing its every need, even though they have little or no experience with dogs. A sick puppy is very like a sick child and should be treated in a similar manner.

If you have a really good dog and you want to prove him at stud and cannot mate him with one of your own bitches, advertise for an approved bitch to be served with a free mating in order to prove your dog. Now you are in a position to advertise your dog at stud, and if he has done some winning and his breeding and temperament are good, you can reasonably expect that he will be booked for services by other breeders.

Those who are not too far away will bring their bitches. This is good from the point of view of a novice, since their practical knowledge will make up for any lack of experience you may still suffer from, and you will get tips from them to add to what you have already learnt. Practical demonstration cannot be learnt from a book.

Bitches sent to you by rail will be better if collected by you at your home town station if it is on a main line. Should it happen that the bitch has to come to a terminus on one line, and be transferred to a different line, it is better to collect at the terminus. I once had a full day of misery. A bitch was expected to arrive at my home town station at two o'clock one afternoon, having arrived at the London Terminus at twelve-fifteen. I went to collect it, but the dog was not there. Telephone messages were sent out to all the likely stations where she might be, but no news. The station from whence the bitch had ben despatched was contacted, and confirmation received that she had been despatched on the 8.15 a.m. train to the London Terminus. I again got in touch with my local station and many times during the day, but the answer was always the same, no livestock here. Time went on and I was getting frantic, thinking perhaps that the crate in which the bitch was travelling had been stolen. As a last resource at about seven-thirty that night I and my son went up to London. Of course, everybody was very busy, but we were given permission to search, after having been told quite definitely that there was no livestock in the goods department. I went one way and he another, looking for a crate we both knew well by sight. At last a welcome exclamation, 'Here she is.' There was the crate underneath a pile of boxes, and on the crate all the necessary details and addresses in very clear writing. Protests were made to the man in charge, but the only reply was, she should have gone on to the station on the label and not been taken into the goods office. We are not responsible. A policeman was fetched and he could only say that if the R.S.P.C.A. were informed they might take the matter up. Fortunately no harm seemed to have been done. As soon as possible she was let out to relieve herself and home she came to a good drink of water and a good meal, long overdue. My advice, therefore, is collect a visiting bitch at a terminus if your station is not on the same line. A bitch belonging to somebody else is a great responsibility and one that is in-season is the greatest of all. Do not, on any account release her unless she has on a collar and lead, and only then, preferably, in an enclosed space from which she cannot escape. It is amazing how quick she can be. If she managed to get away, she would just run and if not caught you would be in terrible trouble with the owner. When you arrive home, if your garden is very secure, let her out for a run.

Being inexperienced it would be better to have a reliable person with you when the mating takes place. I have explained in another chapter how this is best done. Everybody has a different way of doing things and this is one of the easiest and best ways. For the person responsible it is a matter of patience. Let the bitch rest after her mating and return her to her owner the next day if possible, unless, of course, two matings have been arranged. To keep her longer will not only worry the dog but you also. Never, on any account, let your stud dog be sent from his home to serve a bitch, unless in very extreme circumstances when you should accompany him yourself.

Sometimes, for some unknown reason, all your bitches fail to come into season at the times expected and breeding arrangements have to be cancelled. You then start to experiment with new diets and perhaps with drugs prescribed by the veterinary surgeon. Then suddenly all the bitches come into season and being concerned because of the irregularity, you must decide quickly whether to breed from them all and risk being over-run with puppies, or to let some pass and risk having no puppies at all. You must then make a hasty decision, and perhaps make arrangements with the stud owners. You may have had enquiries for dog puppies which requests you hope to fill, and then the bitch has all bitch puppies. Such disappointments and improvisations require patience and courage to sort out. Also you must have self-control so that you do not soar off on glittering golden clouds at a good sale, nor sink into an abyss of gloom when it seems that no one, anywhere, wants to buy a dog.

Most visitors to your kennel will be pleasant normal people, with normal, sensible reasons for wanting a dog; the son's birthday; the wife wants one as a companion, being left alone quite a lot. Other breeders will visit you, often just to see what you can produce and to take a look round to note the conditions of your kennel. Do not think this is just nosiness; it is probably a true interest visit. During that look round they may see a puppy, and as they have an order for a good one which they are not able to fill themselves, yours may fill the order.

Some visitors are very pleasant company and will talk for hours, drink a cup of tea or coffee with you, and whether the business is in pounds or not, you will enjoy the mutual interest in the breed. At these times you can pick up doggy gossip and sometimes be told of possible buyers, or they will tell other people you have some puppies for sale. There are others who come who do not provide a pleasant interlude. They sometimes amuse you, but sometimes disgust you.

Your mail, also, will begin to get quite interesting; perhaps a letter stating

> I just want a Yorkshire to be a companion and a pet . . . I do not wish to show it, but it must have all the essentials of a good dog, such as erect ears, short back, coat of good colour and length, but the price must be reasonable. . . . If you have not a dog to meet my requirements at the moment, please keep my enquiry in mind when you have your next litter.

In fact, a show dog is required at a pet price. This kind of enquiry rarely affects your bank balance, but if you like dogs and people, there will be many temptations to do the unprofitable thing.

There will be the little visitor who will ask politely to see the dogs. He will stand and gaze at the puppies for a time and then ask, 'May I pick one up?' You say, 'Of course you may, if you are very careful. Best to sit on the floor first, then, if the puppy wriggles so much and escapes he hasn't far to fall.' This is good practice with all children, for then there is no fear of the puppy getting hurt. Your visitor by this time will have completely lost his heart. 'I have saved my pocket money for some time and I would so love to have one; how much would it cost?' You think awhile, and then, after summing up how much joy the youngster is going to have with his puppy, agree on a price well within his reach if Mummy and Daddy make up the difference for a birthday present.

There will be lots of telephone calls and lots of queries, but it is so worth it. Sometimes a dear old lady or gentleman who honestly cannot afford much for a pet come along and your heart is softened and off he or she goes with a glint in the eye and a treasure absolutely priceless.

Throughout your breeding career you must search yourself conscientiously for the common complaint known as kennel blindness. The characteristic symptoms of this widespread ailment is the inability to see the faults of your own stock and, in an acute case, the certainty that every other breeders' dogs are no good at all.

Unless previously you have devoted years of study to the breed, you will do most of your real learning during the second five years. By then you will have watched two or maybe three generations develop and will have marked the dominant and recessive traits of your stock. You will also have learned to check pedigrees with a discerning eye and with some awareness of the strong points and the weaknesses of the various bloodlines. You will learn how to make use of them and so develop a puppy which by this time you will have realized comes up to the type you should breed. During those second five years you will experience moments of gratification when someone to whom you have sold a puppy returns to get another, but at the same time you may have moments of frustration when you see an adult who was thought, as a puppy, to be of not much account grown into a really beautiful creature and you would dearly love to buy him back.

Now and then you will wonder if you are still a novice, but not until you realize that a novice is someone who has been breeding not less than six years or for an unlimited amount of time.

Usually, if you have stayed in the breed for the third five years there is no question of wanting to change to another breed however much you may be tempted by a change of fashion in the dog world. Those who have stayed so long know what they are doing and if they discontinue breeding it will be for reasons which have nothing whatever to do with dogs. Often breeders, when they have retired, and no longer have a dog, they straightway go to the shows to see their favourite Yorkshires.

Some people outlive the friends of their youth, lose contact with old friends and neighbours or business associates, but, if you are in the doggy world, your circle of friends will always be spreading rather than contracting, and if you have played fairly and done the best you possibly could for your breed you will find you have done well for yourself.

You will receive welcome and interesting letters and visits from people to whom you have sold dogs, at home, and perhaps abroad. Many mutual and lifelong friends have been made through the sale of a Yorkshire puppy. If you join a dog club it will bring you in contact with people who will be pleasant to know apart from the interest of the club and the breed.

The present Yorkshire Terrier Club was registered on the first day of March in the year 1898 and the Secretary was a Mr J. W. Randall of the Celone, Manchester Road, Thornton Heath, Surrey. He presented a beautiful trophy, which was to be competed for by members of the club, and it is still offered for competition at the Club Championship Show. It is for the second best dog, to be won three times in succession or five times in all.

Before 1914, Mr Dunman was Secretary of the Club and the President Lady Newborough, who resigned in 1933, Lady Edith Windham* filling the vacancy and afterwards becoming Secretary. This office she held until 1946, when she resigned because she was living permanently in Ireland. I was elected Secretary as her successor.

The last Yorkshire Terrier Club Show before the Second World War was held in conjunction with the Richmond Championship Show in 1939, and owing to the discontinuance of Championship shows, a number of small shows were held to try to keep the flag flying. It was not held again until 1946. During the war years members strived to keep their strain and some of the present lovely specimens shown are the offsprings of many of these dogs and are a great credit to some of the older members.

The Yorkshire Terrier lived mostly in the North of England, but at the present time there are as many, if not more, breeders of this exquisite breed in the south. Actresses bought them as pets and popularized them, and foreign visitors to England.

They are now bred in all parts of the world although in very hot climates the heat plays havoc with the beautiful coats. Nevertheless, they still remain popular, living in air-conditioned rooms during the heat.

The Northern Counties Yorkshire Terrier Club was founded in 1947 and in the same year was licensed by the Kennel Club. It held its first meeting at Blackpool Championship Show on 27th June, 1947, when Mrs A. Swan was elected Secretary. The name of the present Secretary will be found in Appendix B.

---

* Later Lady Windham Dawson.

Strains in the Yorkie

In an interesting article written by a well-known judge it was
stated that there was an absence in these days of definite
strains. I do not think this is true of the Yorkshire Terrier,
except where a beginner had got broods from different kennels and mated them to sires regardless of whether his blood-
line suits the bitch or not. There are still some lines that show
there has been a definite breeding plan, and that a policy has
been carried out over the years, for certain types persist. This
is very noticeable in body formation, heads and ears, and
colour, and this seems to run right through families or strains.
By careful outcrossing, coat defects can be eliminated.

When choosing a puppy to run on for showing, these persistent characteristics are very helpful.

A puppy when very young with smutty-looking tan feet (feet
with black and tan mixed) certainly looks as if he can never
develop into the beautiful clear-coloured tan. This is where a
knowledge of the family lines can be a great help and
guidance. Large, floppy, low-placed ears will rarely stand up,
whereas the tiny V-shaped ears which very often the puppy has
erect when born usually remain erect and will give no trouble.
An indifferent tan at maturity is usually heralded by being very
pale at birth. Sometimes when the head is changing from
black it will come up quite silver, but as time goes on the dark
tan can be seen at the roots. The silver grows out and a good
golden tan remains.

The main groups were, in the early history of the breed, in
the Northern counties, Yorkshire, Lancashire, Durham and in
Scotland, and in time drifted down to the south. These dogs
were always noted for their good colour, and the fact that their
coats are more profuse is probably due to the difference in
temperature. Many of the original lines have died out completely and are not very easy to trace as prefixes were not used.
Dogs were known only as Tom, Dick or Harry, but the sire,
Gay Corinthian, five generations back, must be mentioned,
and the bitch, Madge of Arkham, at the same period, both
having perpetuated their quality.

During the last war years there was a complete absence of
Challenge Certificates and there were many beautiful stud

dogs who had no chance of recognition. Invincia Masher was the foremost of these and this broke a long line of champion sires. Ch. Splendor of Invincia was his sire and he was probably the sire of many pre-war champions. Chs. Invincia Gudasgold, Delite of Invincia, and Ch. Eminent, came from this same kennel.

Mr Chips of Yadnum was born during the war, the lovely son of Triagan, son of My Tim, son of Dandy Son, son of Ch. Dandy Duke. Many excellent dogs have been shown from these sires, including the latest Ch. Moon Glow of Yadnum, who is great-grandson of Mr Chips. Ch. Butibel Perseus and a bitch out of him has set the colour in the Scottish Kennel of Johnfield. Nigella of Pagham was a son of Monarch of Harringay, son of that famous Ch. Harringay Remarkable, son of Ch. Mendham Prince. Nigella of Pagham, who unfortunately was not shown during the war years, was the sire of Ch. McKay of Achmonie and Ch. Someone of Achmonie. Ch. Eoforwic Envoy of Yadnum, grandson of Nigella, was the sire of the American Ch. Timothy of Yadnum. Pookshill is another prominent prefix, and Victory Boy, whose sire was Monarch of Harringay, has stamped his excellent colouring on his progeny.

Registration and Transfer

A further revised registration system came into force in 1985. The total number of puppies in the litter must be declared by the breeder and the fee for this 'litter recording' is £5.00 per litter. An additional fee of £5.00 is payable for each named (or registered) puppy, plus £1.00 for each unnamed (not registered) puppy. For example, for a litter of four puppies of which two are registered and two unnamed, the cost will be £5.00 plus £10.00 plus £2.00, total £17.00.

An unnamed puppy from a litter can later be named by the owner for a fee of £5.00.

The name of a registered dog can be changed by an affix holder only (by the addition of the affix) also for a fee of £5.00. This can only be done if the dog has not qualified at a championship show for inclusion in the Kennel Club Stud Register, after which time the name cannot be changed.

If a dog is being sold abroad, an Export Pedigree may be necessary. This can only be obtained from the Kennel Club upon completion of the appropriate application form accompanied by a certificate signed by a Ministry of Agriculture Fisheries and Food veterinary surgeon to the effect that the male dog has two normal testicles fully descended in the scrotum (not necessary for the female). If the puppy is not entire when he is sent abroad, the necessary certification can be obtained from a vet in his new country and forwarded to the Kennel Club with the appropriate fee. The cost of an Export Pedigree is £20.00. When the dog travels he has to be accompanied by a certificate of health completed by your vet. The appropriate form is supplied to him by the Ministry of Agriculture Fisheries and Food. Charges for this examination vary from vet to vet.

Affix

Should you wish to register your own kennel affix, which name is your sole property and exclusive to all dogs owned and registered by you, this can be done by applying to the Kennel Club. The charge for this is £35.00 plus an annual maintenance fee of £10.00. When you complete the application form you will be asked to give three choices of name. These, if not already taken, will be published in the *Kennel Gazette* and objections can be made by anyone with just cause.

Shows

A Championship show is one open to all and where the Kennel Club challenge certificates are awarded to the best dog and the best bitch in the breed. It does not always follow that the dog or bitch winning the first prize in the open classes will be the winner of these certificates, for a dog that has not been beaten in the lower classes can come forward as an unbeaten dog and challenge for the certificate, and if considered by the judge to be the better, gains the award.

Three certificates have to be won by one dog under three different judges before the title of champion can be added to his name. There is also a best of breed certificate, which is given to either the best dog or the best bitch, as the judge decides.

An open show is in all respects the same as a championship show but there are no challenge certificates awarded.

A limited or sanction show is one entirely for members of a club or society. Our breed is benched at the all-breed championship shows, but at the breed club championship shows the society will usually apply to the Kennel Club for exemption, the tables provided for the dogs' show boxes fulfilling the Kennel Club conditions for viewing by the public. Club open and limited shows do not have to be benched, but general canine societies may have to bench if the show is over a certain size.

An exemption show can be run in conjunction with an agricultural show or for the People's Dispensary for Sick Animals, the Animal Health Trust, or some other kind of charity, any profit going to the cause. Permission has to be granted by the Kennel Club to run these shows and a minimum of four classes may be allotted to pedigree dogs, and the remainder to any kind of dog. Even a mongrel can go to one of these shows. They are great fun and often in the children's classes some coming showmen can be seen handling their dogs.

Junior Warrant

This is a certificate issued by the Kennel Club to a dog obtaining 25 points in all before reaching the age of eighteen months. These points are gained at Championship and Open Shows only. The number of points gained at a Championship Show are 3 for a first place award, and at an Open Show, 1 point for a first place award. These points must be gained in Yorkshire Terrier Classes, a first prize in Any Variety Classes does not count. This warrant is not an easy one to win and it is not issued automatically. Application has to be made to the Kennel Club for the appropriate form, completed in respect of the wins, and then if correct, you will receive a Junior Warrant.

Stud Book Number

1978 brought a change in the qualification for Stud Book Number. If the dog is placed first, second or third in the Open Class for the breed at a Championship Show, or is awarded a Challenge Certificate or Reserve Challenge Certificate, he will qualify for a Stud Book Number. The Kennel Club will automatically notify you of the number and it will be published in the *Kennel Gazette*.

Monorchid and Cryptorchid

A monorchid or a cryptorchid is the name given to a dog that is not entire (an entire dog is one which has both testicles fully developed and descended in the scrotum). Monorchidism and cryptorchidism is a show fault in this country at the present time. The Kennel Club have changed the show rule regarding this in recent years.

The testicles develop first behind the kidneys and from there they slowly descend into the scrotum. Sometimes at three months they can be seen, but some dogs mature much later and if there is any doubt about a dog you are selling, consult your vet. He is the one who has to sign the form for an export certificate.

In America dogs have been operated on successfully to bring the testicle down.

Travelling to Shows

If you are the proud possessor of a show dog and you wish to travel by rail to a show some distance away, you can travel your dog in his show case free of charge, provided the show case is within the required size stated by the railways. If however you travel with the dog on your lap, you will have to buy a ticket for him. The charge for this is usually the cost of an adult single fare.

In some areas, coach parties are arranged. These are usually much cheaper than rail travel and you will be with other doggie people, travelling to the show ground from various pick-up points. Details of such coach parties can be found in many championship show schedules and sometimes in the dog press.

If you are planning to take your pet on holiday, it is a good idea to get him used to a box or basket so that he will travel without getting too excited. If you are going by train and he is not a good traveller, you can clean him up without disturbing other passengers and he will have his bed with him. It is, of course, much safer to have him boxed when travelling in a car. If the vehicle is involved in an accident he cannot escape. Also in a hotel if anyone should come into your room, the same will apply.

Quarantine

A dog being imported into the British Isles has to go straight to a quarantine kennel, licensed by the Government. There he has to stay for six months, is fed, exercised and taken care of in every detail. His health is watched by the veterinary surgeon in charge. The various kennels differ in their charges and at the end of six months the bill can be a very heavy one. It is better to pay either weekly or monthly. The law compelling dogs imported into the British Isles to go into quarantine is especially hard on people who have been living abroad and have brought their pet with them. Of course, he can be visited quite frequently and by seeing his master he will not fret so much. I once knew a little Yorkshire Terrier who had to stay at the Hackbridge Quarantine Kennels, her mistress travelling down from London each day to see her. At first the dog was miserable, but after a time she got to know when her mistress would arrive and would wait patiently for her.

The reason for quarantine in the British Isles is to try to keep our country free from rabies, that dreadful scourge that attacks both dog and man. There have been a few confirmed cases of rabies over the last eighty years, mostly animals in quarantine, and some hefty fines have been imposed on those who have tried to avoid the quarantine regulations. Anyone having consideration for their dog and other people should be

pleased to keep their animal in a registered kennel for the
required six months.

Regarding the Law

How many dog owners appreciate their legal liabilities? There
are a number of laws which apply to dog ownership. They are
intended to protect dogs from cruelty and misuse, to protect
domestic livestock and wild animals and to protect your
neighbours from your dog causing them annoyance.

Some local authorities make their own bye-laws concerning
the fouling of footpaths, keeping your dog on a lead in public
parks, not allowing dogs on beaches or not allowing dogs to go
into certain public buildings.

Many restaurants and food shops prohibit dogs from their
premises in accordance with the Food Hygiene Regulations
which came out in 1970. The Forestry Commission have their
own bye-laws concerning the preservation of wildlife and
birds and before taking your dog onto such land find out what
these are.

Your dog must not cause annoyance to your neighbour by
prolonged barking or trespassing on his land so make sure
that your fencing is secure. Your dog must wear a collar at all
times when outside your property, bearing your address, the
only exceptions to this being gundogs and working dogs.

Licences

If you are involved in any of the activities mentioned below
you will require a licence from your local authority:

The Breeding of Dogs Act 1973   Owners of more than two
bitches from which puppies are bred for sale require a
licence.

Boarding Establishment Act 1963   If you board dogs for pay-
ment, whether you do this as a private house or a kennel, you
require a licence.

Pet Animals Act 1951   You may be required to take out this licence if you buy puppies for resale or breed a number of puppies for sale whether your premises is a conventional shop or not.

Selling dogs   Dogs and puppies must not be sold in the street or any public place, or to a child under 12 years of age, or in conjunction with a rag or old clothes dealing business.

Sale of Goods Act 1979   It is generally accepted that livestock is bought as seen, but if the buyer states that the puppy is required for a specific purpose e.g. for breeding or showing, and in due course the dog does not fulfil that purpose, under the Sale of Goods Act it may be regarded as an offence and the purchaser may have a claim. If a pedigree is given with a puppy it must be correct. It may be regarded as obtaining money by false pretences to given an incorrect pedigree.

Licence   In 1867 an Act was passed stating that anyone owning a puppy over six months of age should buy a licence. In 1986 Parliament decided that it was now impractical to collect the small cost of such a licence and decided to do away with it, but at the time of writing this has not yet been legislated upon and until that time one is still obliged to buy a licence to keep a dog.

For the Sick or Lost

The People's Dispensary for Sick Animals is a wonderful organization for providing the necessary attention needed for the recovery to health of the sick dog, in fact any animal, bird or reptile. There is usually a surgery in each of the large towns all over the country. No fees are charged and the animal will receive as much care and attention as if he had been taken to the most expensive veterinary surgeon, so if you have a sick dog and really cannot afford to pay the usual vet's fee, go along and have him treated for just a trifle, and put what you can afford in their collecting-box. The attendants, and all concerned with the P.D.S.A., are a wonderful lot of people, kind and understanding.

The late Duchess of Hamilton opened her beautiful house

near Shaftesbury, now called the Fern Sanctuary, to accommodate dogs who, through some ill-fortune, are homeless. Here they are fed and cared for by a band of workers until another home can be found for them.

Another great institution which has done a most excellent humane work is worthy of support of all lovers of dogs; it is the Dogs' Home at Battersea, London. The work of housing temporarily lost and starving dogs and attending to dogs that are in ill-health was started in the nineteenth century and it has expanded greatly due to the increase in the work that it carries out. Nearly 100 years ago a Member of the House of Lords raised the question of the care of the dog, but his remarks were met with scorn. The poor dog had very few friends at that time. The loyalty and fidelity of dog to man was no less strong then, than it is now, but it was left to the gentle sex to get something going. It so happened that an ill dog was found on a door-step and passed by many people, but one dog-lover, a Mrs Tealby, stopped. The situation gave her an idea, that of taking some practical steps for providing the poor thing with shelter. She, together with a friend, a Mrs Major, took the first steps towards the founding of a permanent institution for the protection of lost and starving dogs. A temporary home was started in a very quiet and small way in October 1860.

In November of the same year at the offices of the R.S.P.C.A. the first meeting was held, and the scheme got well on the way. In 1879 the home was visited by his Royal Highness the Prince of Wales, accompanied by the Queen of the Belgians, both expressing pleasure and approval of the working and the general management of the institution.

Queen Victoria honoured the institution by becoming its patron and subscribed annually to the funds. It was her express wish and special desire that the then three-day period, for the keeping of dogs not claimed, should be extended to five days, before consigning them to the lethal chamber. Now when I hear the song 'Underneath the Arches' I think of the home, because it is actually underneath railway arches.

In April 1905, five railways arches and a large strip of land adjoining became vacant. These were acquired and converted into a spacious range of kennels with roomy exercising yards, and at the same time the old house was reconstructed. This work included new drainage as well as new well-ventilated kennels, electricity was installed, and everything that would make the place hygienic and comfortable for the dogs was done.

The work carried on at the Home consists of tending sick dogs at a nominal charge, restoring lost dogs to their owners, providing temporary shelter and food for starving and home-less dogs, and endeavouring to find homes for healthy ones at a small charge. I have known several dogs who were bought at the Home. They have all been good guards and wonderful pets; one, a Pekingese is now fifteen years old. A merciful and painless death is ensured for the old, those injured beyond repair, and the dangerous.

All dogs lost in the London and Greater London area are taken from the police stations (the police are the only body authorized to seize stray dogs) to the Home, where they stay for a period of seven days before they are sold or disposed of. This enables anyone who has lost a dog in the London area to enquire if it has been found, and claim it. When lost dogs arrive they are registered with a distinctive number. There may be several of the same description and it is impossible for the officials to undertake identification from a verbal or written description, so the owner must go along and claim his own dog. This is a good thing, because it gives one the opportunity of going round the kennels to make a thorough search. The officials are always very glad to render every possible assistance.

The Home still has a royal patron in our Queen, Elizabeth II, but with all the enlargements and improvements the Home is always in need of support.

CONCLUSION

Nearly every Briton loves a dog and in millions of homes the dog is treated as a member of the family. All over the world some species of animal is loved, respected, or idolized, but here in this island home of ours it is the dog. At heart it does not really matter what kind of dog he is, as any one of them who gets his feet under our tables is there for keeps. Some may faintly regret that he is too large, or too small, too boisterous, or idle and stupid, or some other complaint is made of him, but when he is in, he is in, and he is spoilt and cosseted. The owner will, perhaps, bore his friends with stories of his charm or his great intelligence, and will protect him from criticism with all the power of his convictions.

This state of affairs is by no means new, it has been going on for centuries, but what is comparatively new is that more and more want to own, not just a dog, but one with a known line of antecedents and a readily identifiable appearance, in fact a pedigree dog. It has been said that it is a mere matter of snob appeal, another method of 'keeping up with the Joneses'.

It is unfortunately true that some film stars choose pets that are fashionable and photogenic, regardless of their suitability. One has no idea what a mongrel puppy will look like when he is a year old, or what size he will be when mature. As for his character, well, that's in the lap of the gods, but with a pedigree dog, almost as soon as his eyes are open, one can tell how he will look when mature, although the finer points cannot always be assessed. One knows by the group to which the dog belongs whether he will be small, medium or large, or whether he will possess the desired temperament. It is generally thought that a pedigree dog has a better temperament, but it is not really that it is so much better, but that it is more predictable. Nevertheless, some mongrels are the most devoted of pets with temperaments as sweet as dogs of excellent pedigrees. So good luck to every dog-lover, whatever his choice of breeding.

YORKSHIRE TERRIER
REGISTRATION TOTALS AT THE KENNEL
CLUB

1950	1217
1951	1331
1952	1241
1953	1248
1954	1462
1955	1708
1956	2148
1957	2313
1958	2824
1959	3244
1960	3863
1961	4385
1962	4908
1963	5130
1964	5531
1965	6129
1966	6306
1967	7389
1968	8842
1969	10,212
1970	11,016
1971	10,577
1972	12,832
1973	13,780
1974	15,147
1975	14,640
1976	7817
1977	5428
1978	12,618
1979	19,187
1980	17,333
1981	14,149
1982	12,755
1983	12,407
1984	11,788
1985	12,141
1986	10,637

APPENDIX B

YORKSHIRE TERRIER CLUBS

THE YORKSHIRE TERRIER CLUB
Hon. Sec.: Mrs B. F. Whitbread,
13, Weltmore Road, Luton, Beds.

THE MIDLAND YORKSHIRE TERRIER CLUB
Hon. Sec.: Mrs K. Naylor,
Holly Cottage, 356 Lichfield Road, Burntwood, Staffs.

THE NORTHERN COUNTIES YORKSHIRE TERRIER CLUB
Hon. Sec.: Mr A. Blamires,
482, Bradford Road, Brighouse, West Yorkshire, HD6 4ED.

THE SOUTH WESTERN YORKSHIRE TERRIER CLUB
Hon. Sec.: Mrs I. Millard,
6, St. Andrews Road, Backwell, Bristol, Avon, BS19 3NR.

THE YORKSHIRE TERRIER CLUB OF SCOTLAND
Hon. Sec.: Mrs M. Rillie,
129, St. Quivox Road, Prestwick, Ayrshire.

THE ULSTER YORKSHIRE TERRIER CLUB
Hon. Sec.: Mrs M. Lamont,
65, Old Dundonald Road, Belfast, BT16 OXS.

THE EASTERN YORKSHIRE TERRIER CLUB
Hon. Sec.: Mrs M. Millward,
Sanbar, Main Road, South Reston, Lincs, LN11 8JQ.

YORKSHIRE TERRIER CLUB OF SOUTH WALES
Hon. Sec.: Mr M. D. Owens,
29, Rhydyffynnon, Pontyates, Llanelli, Dyfed, SA15 5UG.

CHESHIRE AND NORTH WALES YORKSHIRE TERRIER SOCIETY
Hon. Sec.: Mrs P. Grunnil,
16, Brook Lane, Chester, CH2 2AP.

LINCOLN AND HUMBERSIDE YORKSHIRE TERRIER CLUB
Hon. Sec.: Mr B. Shirley,
Windmill Bungalow, Bucknall, Lincs, LN3 5EB.

The above information was correct at the time of going to press, but confirmation of the details can be obtained from The Kennel Club, 1, Clarges Street, Piccadilly, London, W1Y 8AB.

APPENDIX C

CUPS TO BE WON BY MEMBERS AT THE YORKSHIRE TERRIER CLUB'S CHAMPIONSHIP SHOW

The Phirno Cup Presented by Miss P. I. Noakes for best special puppy.

The Westbrook Challenge Cup Presented for best special puppy bitch.

The Versatile Cup Presented by Mr Hughes for best puppy dog.

The Achmonie Cup Presented by Miss P. Marter for best puppy bitch.

The President's Challenge Bowl Presented for the best puppy in show.

The Yadnum Trophy Presented by the late Mrs E. Munday for the best junior dog.

The Astolat Cup Presented by the late Mrs Charlton Haw for best special yearling dog.

The St. Louis Challenge Cup Presented by the late Messrs J. P. Martin and R. Marshall for the best novice dog.

The Russell Cup Presented by the late Mrs J. Russell for the best graduate dog.

The Sprig of Blossom Cup Presented by the late Mr Marshall for the best limit dog.

The Deanchel Trophy Presented by the late Mrs E. Taylor for the best open dog.

The Whisperdales Cup Presented by the late Mr R. Wardill for the best junior bitch.

The Batsford Memorial Cup Presented for the best special yearling bitch.

The Mitchell Challenge Cup Presented by the late Mr Mitchell for the best novice bitch.

The Pomeroywoods Cup Presented by Mr and Mrs A. Wood for the best graduate bitch.

The Butibel Cup Presented by the late Mrs J. Russell for the best post graduate bitch.

152

The Soham Challenge Cup Presented by the late Lady Edith Windham Dawson for the best limit bitch.

The Ch. Ozmilion Justimagine Cup Presented by Mr O. A. Sameja for the best limit bitch.

The Wildweir Trophy Presented by Mrs J. Gordon and Miss J. Bennett for the best open bitch.

The Tomkins Cup Presented by the late Mr G. Tomkins for the dog challenge certificate winner.

The Jacaranda Trophy Presented by Mrs J. Montgomery for the dog reserve challenge certificate winner.

The Ch. Madam Butterfly Cup Presented by the late Mrs Richardson for the winner of the bitch challenge certificate.

The Soham Cup Presented by the late Lady Edith Windham Dawson for the bitch reserve challenge certificate winner.

The Witchell Bowl Presented by Miss H. Flint for the best in show.

The Lady Newborough Cup Presented by the late Lady Newborough for the best opposite sex to best in show.

The Japanese Cup Presented for the best dog or bitch bred by exhibitor.

The Belona Bowl Presented by the late Mrs J. Russell for the best brood bitch.

The Rutland Cup Presented by Mrs Beeson for the best brood bitch.

APPENDIX D

BRITISH YORKSHIRE TERRIER CHAMPIONS, 1947 to 1986

Name of Champion	Sex	Sire	Dam	Breeder	Owner	Date of Birth
1947:						
Bens Blue Pride	D	Blue Flash	Jill	Mr Roper	Mr Williamson	8.7.44
Lady Nada	B	Wee Willie Winkle	Little Flower	Mrs R. Allen	Mrs Hebson	9.9.42
1948:						
Hebsonian Jealousy	B	Gay Prince	Hebsonian Harana	Mrs Hebson	Mrs Hebson	10.3.49
Veeplustoo of Achmonie	B	Sweet Memory of Achmonie	Isolda of Achmonie	Miss Macdonald	Miss Macdonald	9.5.45
Starlight	D	Marten Teddy	Adora	Mr Orford	Mrs Hargreaves	15.10.45
1949:						
Wee Don of Atherleigh	D	Don Progress	Beauty of Atherleigh	Mr Hayes	Mr Hayes	13.9.45
McCay of Achmonie	D	Nigella of Pagham	Sophie of Achmonie	Miss Macdonald	Miss Macdonald	21.4.46
Splendour of Invincia	D	Invincia Masher	Olie of Invincia	Mrs Swan	Mrs Swan	16.7.47
Vemair Parkview Preview	D	Parkview Prince	Parkview Dinky	Mr Bain	Mrs Mair	12.5.46
Tufty of Johnstounburn	B	Midge's Pal	Hazy of Johnstounburn	Mrs Crookshank	Mrs Crookshank	3.5.45

154

1950:

Name						
Blue Dolly	B	Ch. Bens Blue Pride	Little Marionette	Mr Coates	Mr Coates	2.4.46
Mr Pimm of Johnstounburn	D	Parkview Prince	Flea of Johnstounburn	Mr Sturrock	Mrs Crookshank	29.2.47
Dinah Beau	B	Bridle Copper King	Beauty of Atherleigh	Mr Hayes	Miss Hartley	24.6.48
Winpal Arine	B	Soham Caryle	Anita of Soham	Lady E. Windham Dawson	Miss Palmer	13.2.47

1951:

Name						
Wee Gertrude	B	Monican Punch	Queenie's Pride	Mr Thurlow	Mrs Chard and Miss Fairchild	16.1.48
Feona of Phylreyne	B	Christoeferobin of Phylreyne	Phylreyne Irrepressible	Mrs Raine	Mrs Raine	12.2.48
Vemair Principal Boy	D	Parkview Prince	Frosty of Johnstounburn	Mr Bain	Mrs Mair	28.6.49
Sorreldene Honey Son of the Vale	D	Harringay Little Dandy	Pretty Paulette	Mrs Sharpe	Mrs Bradley	25.11.48
Hopwood Camelia	B	Invincia Masher	Invincia Margretta	Mrs Swan	Miss Martin	9.3.48
Wee Blue Atom	D	Little Blue Boy	Our Sue	Mr Latliff	Mrs Overett	20.7.48
Martinwyns Golden Girl	B	Martin Teddy	Marian Martinette	Mr Coates	Mrs Montgomery	24.4.48
Martinwyns Surprise of Atherleigh	D	Invincia Masher	Pat of Atherleigh	Mr Hayes	Mr Coates	24.11.47

BRITISH YORKSHIRE TERRIER CHAMPIONS

Name of Champion	Sex	Sire	Dam	Breeder	Owner	Date of Birth
1952:						
Adora of Invincia	B	Invincia Masher	Ollie of Invincia	Mrs Swan	Mrs Swan	5.6.48
Tatinia of Invincia	B	Pride of Invincia	Nancy of Invincia	Mrs Swan	Mrs Stirk	25.9.48
Sunstar of Invincia	D	Invincia Masher	Margie of Invincia	Mrs Swan	Mrs Swan	5.6.50
Blue Belle	B	Wee Blue Atom	Blue Bonnet	Miss Noakes	Miss Noakes	21.8.50
Someone of Achmonie	D	Ch. McCay of Achmonie	Fiona of Achmonie	Miss Macdonald	Miss Macdonald	—
Wee Eve of Yadnum	B	Ch. Mr Pimm of Johnstounburn	Scotford Queen	Mr Scott	Mrs Munday	10.8.51
Kelsboro Quality Boy	D	Gayways Little Trotters	Dinkie Blue	Mrs Cross	Mrs Cross	28.6.49
Firhill Fairy	B	Midge's Pal	Miss Monty	Mr Anderson	Mrs Pannett	30.9.48
Winpal Henriella	B	Henry of Soham	Prunella of Achmonie	Miss Macdonald	Miss Palmer	30.3.49
Jacaranda Beauty	B	Little Blue Boy	Bridle Sweetbriar	Mrs Montgomery	Mrs Montgomery	25.1.51
1953:						
Vemair Spider	D	Midge's Pal	Coogee Dinah	Mr Johnstone	Mrs Mair	30.9.48

Martinwyns Debonaire	D	Little Blue Boy	Our Sue	Mr Latliff	Mr Coates	4.10.49
Medium of Johnstounburn	B	Midge's Pal	Misty of Johnstounburn	Mrs Crookshank	Mrs Crookshank	23.10.50
Aerial of Winpal	B	Prince Cosmo of Winpal	Ch. Winpal Arine	Miss Palmer	Miss Palmer	4.7.52
Eoforwic Envoy of Yadnum	D	Blue Guinea of Yadnum	Florentina of Yadnum	Mrs Prosser	Mrs Munday	1.7.50
Jessica of Westridge	B	Martinwyns Surprise of Atherleigh	Pauline of Westridge	Mr Grist	Mr Grist	19.7.51
Stirkean Chota Sahib	D	Splendour of Invincia	Empress of Invincia	Mrs Swan	Mrs Stirk	22.8.51
Butibel Perseus	D	Bowdigan Prince Charming	Lovely Blue Princess	Mrs Russell	Mrs Russell	20.11.49
1954:						
Midnight Gold of Yadnum	D	Pip the Piper	Lady Prudence of Yadnum	Mrs Donaldson	Mrs Munday	29.4.53
Myrtle of Johnstounburn	B	Mr Pimm of Johnstounburn	Misty of Johnstounburn	Mrs Crookshank	Mrs Crookshank	8.7.49
Faye of Phylreyne	B	Sorreldene Honeyson of the Vale	Fiona of Phylreyne	Mrs Raine	Mrs Raine	10.4.52
1955:						
Burghwallis Little Nip	D	Burghwallis Waggie	Stanhope Queen	Mr Howard	Mrs Betton	29.6.52
Sehow Independent	B	Paghan Sehow Special	Pennywort of Pagham	Miss Marter	Miss Howes	18.5.53

BRITISH YORKSHIRE TERRIER CHAMPIONS

Name of Champion	Sex	Sire	Dam	Breeder	Owner	Date of Birth
Wadeholme Little Mitzi	B	Peddler Boy	Sehow Hopeful	Mrs Drake	Mrs Wade	19.12.52
Stirkean Kandy Boy	D	Ch. Stirkean Chota Sahib	Trix of Invincia	Mrs Stirk	Mrs Stirk	23.12.53
Martinwyns Adora	B	Martinwyns Teddy	Wee Suzetta	Mrs Latliff	Mrs Seymour	25.1.53
Eppertone Bon Ton	D	Eppertone Surprise	Mam's Little Pal	Mrs Read	Mrs Hill	5.6.53
Vemair Uncle Sam	D	Ch. Vemair Principal Boy	Nemorosa Jill	Mr Hall	Mrs Mair	4.7.52
Eastgrove Gay Boy	D	Gayways Little Trotters	Susan's Wee Lady	Mr Ford	Mrs Hargreaves	14.1.52
Delia of Erlcour	B	Victory Boy	Miretta Marianne	Mrs Batsford	Mrs Batsford	10.6.53
Blue Symon	D	Golden Fame	Dinah is Good	Miss Armstrong	Mrs John	29.9.51
1956:						
Pipit of Johnstounburn	B	Ch. Mr Pimm of Johnstounburn	Pixy of Johnstounburn	Mrs Crookshank	Mrs Crookshank	6.9.54
Burantheas Angel Bright	B	Ch. Mr Pimm of Johnstounburn	Buranthea Paris Jewel	Mrs Burfield	Mrs Burfield	29.4.54

Name		Sire	Dam			Date
Hilaire of Pookshill	D	Starlight of Pookshill	Rosalinda of Erlcour	Mrs Batsford	Mrs Wood	23.1.54
Moon Glow of Yadnum	D	Sir Gay of Yadnum	Pretty Paulette	Mrs Sharpe	Mrs Munday	13.6.55
Aureola of Winpal	B	Butibel Mercury	Aimee of Winpal	Miss Palmer	Miss Palmer	24.10.52
1957:						
Cressida of Erlcour	B	Dandini of Erlcour	Miretta Marianne	Mrs Batsford	Mrs Batsford	22.4.56
Martini	B	Ch. Splendour of Invincia	Cherie of Invincia	Mrs Swan	Mrs Beech	1.8.53
Blue Orchid of Hilfore	B	Totis Treasure	Midget of Hilfore	Mrs Seymour	Mrs Seymour	8.8.55
Prim of Johnstounburn	B	Ch. Mr Pimm of Johnstounburn	Lady of the Lake	Mr Brown	Mrs Rossiter	25.7.55
Pimbron of Johnstounburn	D	Ch. Mr Pimm of Johnstounburn	Lady of the Lake	Mr Brown	Mrs Crookshank	4.7.54
Symons Querida of Tolestar	B	Blue Symon	Honey Queen	Mrs John	Mrs Tole	16.9.54
1958:						
Bystander's Replica	D	The Young Aristocrat	Jill	Miss S. Logan	Miss S. Logan	22.8.54
Coulgorm Chloe	B	Coulgorm Remus	Versatile Veronica	Mr A. Hughes	Mrs C. Hutchin	10.5.56
Deebees Stirkean's Faustina	B	Stirkean's Chota Sahib Ch.	Stirlean's Astolat Enchantress	Mrs E. A. Stirk	Mrs S. D. Beech	15.2.57
June's Boy	D	Little Blue Boy	Dainty Princess Suzanne	Mrs E. F. Latliff	Mr J. Latliff	19.10.53

APPENDIX D—cont.

BRITISH YORKSHIRE TERRIER CHAMPIONS

Name of Champion	Sex	Sire	Dam	Breeder	Owner	Date of Birth
Kavelin Gaiety Boy	D	Ravelin Golden Boy	Chingford Sweet Sue	Mrs E. F. Latliff	Miss P. I. Noakes	13.10.55
Sir Lancelot of Astolat	D	Pagham Sehow Special	Astolat Nicolette	Mrs P. Charlton Haw	Mrs P. Charlton Haw	6.2.56
Societyrow Dog Friday	D	Fawn of Fiskerton	Lassie of Societyrow	Mrs J. Barrs	Mr and Mrs E. Barrs	27.4.56
Sturkean's Rhapsody	D	Shirkean's Chota Sahib Ch.	Sturkean's Anne Marie of Winpal	Mrs E. A. Stirk	Mrs E.A. Stirk	21.2.57
1959:						
Buranthea's Doutelle	D	Mr Pimm of Johnstounburn Ch. (& I. Ch.)	Buranthea's York Sensation	Mrs H. D. Burfield	Mrs H. D. Burfield	8.5.57
Don Carlos of Progreso	D	Martynwyns Wee Teddy Ch.	Shirlorn Sally	Mrs C. Hutchin	Mrs C. Hutchin	20.12.57
Elaine of Astolat	B	Pagham Sehow Special	Astolat Nicolette	Mrs P. Charlton Haw	Mrs P. Charlton Haw	6.2.56
Pagnell Prima Donna of Wiske	B	Burghwallis Little Nip Ch.	Prism of Johnstounburn	Mrs S. I. Groom	Mrs K. M. Renton	1.5.57
Pedimins Piper	D	Bonclad of Invincia	Pedimins Parade	Mr G. Porter	Mr G. Porter	22.10.57

160

Stirkean's Astonoff Horatio	D	Stirkean's Teekhai	Astonoff Victory Victorios	Mrs M. Etherington	Mrs E. A. Stirk	31.3.58

1960:

Deebees Campari	D	Stirkean's Chota Sahib Ch.	Deebees Lillet	Mrs S. D. Beech	Mrs S. D. Beech	1.5.59
Burghwallis Vikki	D	Burghwallis Little Nip Ch.	Prism of Johnstounburn	Mrs S. I. Groom	Mrs M. Betton	1.5.57
Hampark Dandy	D	Ear-Wi-Go of Tzumiao	Chota Memsahib	Mr R. Wilkinson	Mr W. Wilkinson	26.6.58
My Sweet Susanne	B	Totis Treasure	Gloria's Girl	Mrs D. R. Baynes	Mrs D. R. Baynes	24.6.58
Sungold of Supreme	B	Happy Warrior of Saughey	Tauntsom Polly Anna	Mr D. A. Smith	Mr D. A. Smith	22.5.58
Wadeholme Happy Quest	D	Wadeholme Staraza of Clu-Mor	Wadeholme Merry Maid	Mrs L. J. Wade	Mrs L. J. Wade	12.7.57

1961:

Adora Junior of Hilfore	D	Ravelin Golden Boy	Marrynwyns Adora Ch.	Mrs V. Seymour	Mr H. T. Seymour	30.7.58
Burghwallis Brideen	B	Burghwallis Little Nip Ch.	Litte Sheba	Mrs A. Brown	Mrs M. Betton	15.2.58
Deebees Isa La Bela	B	Stirkean's Chota Sahib Ch.	Deebees Lillet	Mrs S. D. Beech	Mrs S. D. Beech	1.5.59
Doone of Wiske	B	Burghwallis Sukyboy	Madcap Molly	Mr W. Quinn	Mrs K. M. Renton	12.3.59

BRITISH YORKSHIRE TERRIER CHAMPIONS

Name of Champion	Sex	Sire	Dam	Breeder	Owner	Date of Birth
Fuchia of Fiskerton	B	Fiskerton Limelight of Lilactime	Stirkean's Frisky Dot	Mrs V. Moyes	Mrs V. Moyes	26.3.58
Glamour Boy of Glengonner	D	Little Tot of Glengonner	Queen of Birkburn	Mr A. Bennie	Mr D. A. Peck	11.6.59
Leyam Mascot	D	June's Boy Ch.	Kim's Starlight	Mrs D. Mayell	Mrs D. Mayell	31.12.58
Mammas's Little Topper	D	Beechrise Dandy	Hallowe'en of Grenbar	Mr J. Walker	Mrs K. H. Cherryholme	20.7.58
Progress of Progreso	D	Don Carlos of Progreso Ch.	Coulgorm Chloe Ch.	Mrs C. Hutchin	Mrs C. Hutchin	2.4.59
Stirkean's Puff Puffin	B	Stirkean's Chota Sahib Ch.	Stirkean's Astolats Enchantress	Mrs E. A. Stirk	Mrs E. A. Stirk	18.5.58
1962:						
Deebees Hot Toddy	D	Deebees Campari Ch.	Deebees Phoebe	Mrs S. D. Beech	Mrs S. D. Beech	9.6.60
Elmslade Galahad of Yadnum	D	Elsmlade Chuffty	Elmslade Moon Maiden	Mrs M. Slade	Mrs E. Munday	11.8.60
Guyton's Spring Blossom	B	Bonnies Apple Blossom	Our Pepita	Mr G. Kniveton	Mr G. Kniveton	17.5.60

Jacaranda Blue Mischief	B	Jacaranda Jolly Boy	Jacaranda Petite	Mrs J. Montgomery	Mrs J. Montgomery	1.2.61
Kelsbro Blue Pete	D	Kelsbro Brigadier	Kelsbro Pretty Peggy	Mr H. Cross	Mr H. Cross	6.11.59
Melody Maker of Embyll	B	Don Carlos of Progreso Ch.	Little Blue Wonder	Mr W. E. Everitt	Mrs C. Hutchin	11.12.59
Pontana Prodigy Dainty	B	Pedimins Prodigy	Tulip Design	Mr G. Howells	Mr G. Howells	9.12.60
'Stirkean's Mr Tims	D	Stirkean's Titmouse	Stirkean Krakawin	Mrs E.Stirk	Mrs E. Stirk	13.5.60
Sundance of Wiske	B	Burghwallis Vikki	Vanessa of Wiske	Mrs K. M. Renton	Mrs K. M. Renton	18.8.59
1963:						
Charm of Wadeholme	B	Wadeholme Staraza of Clu Mor	Wadeholme Wee Rebel	Mrs L. J. Wade	Mrs L. J. Wade	7.10.59
Deebees Caromia	B	Deebees Hot Toddy Ch.	Deebees Invincia Rosemary	Mrs S. D. Beech	Mrs S. D. Beech	7.11.61
Hopwood Desireable	D	Hopwood Torville Majestic	Hopwood Fantasia	Miss E. Martin	Mr J. W. Hutchinson	8.3.59
Pagnell Peter Pan	D	Burghwallis Little Nip Ch.	Prism of Johnstoun-burn	Mrs S. I. Groom	Mrs S. I. Groom	17.10.61
Tzumiao's Cheetah of Martinez	B	Ear-Wi-Go of Tzumiao	Victoria's Pride	Mr & Mrs J. Martin	Mrs E. Gilbert	25.5.60
Wenscoes Wendolene	B	Ear-Wi-Go of Tzumiao	Pedimins Proposal	Miss W. A. Schofield	Miss W. A.Schofield *(now Mrs W. A. Whiteley)*	26.5.61

BRITISH YORKSHIRE TERRIER CHAMPIONS

Name of Champion	Sex	Sire	Dam	Breeder	Owner	Date of Birth
Yorkfold Wrupertbear	D	Yorkfold Chocolate Boy	Yorkfold Koala	Mrs D. Rossiter	Mrs D. Rossiter	6.9.61
1964:						
Burantheas Saint Malachy	D	Piccolo Patrico	Buranthea Doutelle Replica	Mrs H. D. Burfield	Mrs H. D. Burfield	25.11.60
Deebees Little Dodo	B	Deebees Stirkeans Drummer Boy	Deebees Prunella of Invincia	Mrs S. D. Beech	Mrs S. D. Beech	11.2.62
Goodiff Blue Dragon	D	Hampark Dandy Ch.	Trixie of Winpal	Mr M. G. Taylor	Mr G. Crowther	6.10.61
Millfield Mandy	B	Pagnell Brigadier	Solandra Blue Binky	Mrs C. Bailey	Mrs M. Hepworth	9.3.62
Minerva of Johnstoun- burn	B	Pinbron of Johnstounburn Ch	Muffit of Johnstounburn	Mrs M. U. Crook- shank	Mrs M. D. Lowrie	9.10.61
Phirno Magic Moment	B	Ravelin Gaiety Boy Ch.	Phirno Miss Mandy	Miss P. Noakes	Miss P. Noakes	12.9.62
Progreso Lover Boy	D	Progress of Progreso Ch.	Pink Gin of Progreso	Mrs C. Hutchin	Mrs C. Hutchin	14.1.62
Romance of Wiske	B	Templevale Pertin- acious	Miss Bessie Boo	Mrs J. R. Milnes	Mrs K. M. Renton	2.10.62

Skyrona Blue Prince	D	Baby Peachy of Rosehara	Woldsdene Blue Rose	Mrs G. Sykes	15.7.62
Yorkfold McPickle	D	Buranthea's Saint Malachy Ch.	Gold Dinky of Arcady	Mrs D. Rossiter	17.5.62
Golden Button of Yadnum	B	Emperor of Yadnum	Bonny Blue of Yadnum	Mrs E. Munday	7.5.61
1965:					
Anston Cindy Loo	B	Anston Blue Emperor	Alfeebas Joy	Mrs A. L. Buxton	29.2.60
My Precious Joss	D	Pimbrom of Johnstounburn Ch.	Bonny Jean	Mrs C. Flockhart	21.2.63
Ruswel Chorus Girl of Brendali	B	Glamour Boy of Glengonner Ch.	Mandy of Glengonner	Mr D. A. Peck	20.8.62
Templevale Niaissmo of Wiske	B	Templevale Benissimo	Templevale Lady Monia	Mrs L. H. Briggs	11.7.63
Viada Rosina	B	Wylhylda Tiny Tim	Sadie of Invincia	Mrs V. A. Monger	15.8.63
Wedgwoods Starmist	D	Fair Victor of Clu Mor	Wedgewood's Vickey	Mrs C. L Morris	4.5.62
Whisperdales Phirno Carmen	B	Ravelin Gaiety Boy Ch.	Blue Biddy	Miss P. I. Noakes	26.2.63
1966:					
Carlwyns Wee Teddy Toff	D	Ch. Stirkeans Astenoffs Horatio	Stirkeans Cherry Ripe	Mrs W. E. Nichols	7.10.63

APPENDIX D—cont.

BRITISH YORKSHIRE TERRIER CHAMPIONS

Name of Champion	Sex	Sire	Dam	Breeder	Owner	Date of Birth
Phirno St. George	D	Ravelin Little Jimmy	Phirno Dawn Delight	Miss P. Noakes	Miss P. Noakes	23.4.64
Skyrona Blue Girl	B	Ch. Skyrona Blue Prince	Woldsdene Blue Rose	Mrs G. Sykes	Mrs G. Sykes	22.6.64
Templevale Jessica of Wiske	B	Templevale Simonson	Templevale Giselle	Mrs L. H. Briggs	Mrs K. M. Renton	17.10.64
Beechrise Superb	D	Ch. Pagnell Peter Pan	Beechrise Pixie	Mrs H. Griffiths	Mrs H. Griffiths	5.8.63
Dorrit's Leyam Scampie	D	Leyam Tuppence	Leyam Starbright	Mrs D. Mayell	Mrs D. Baynes	19.11.62
Progreso Pearl	B	Progreso Melody Son	Fairmead Jane	Mr Brown	Mrs C. Hutchin	2.7.64
Lillyhill Pimbronette	B	Ch. Pimbron of Johnstounburn	Fair Blossom	Mr W. Dores	Mrs W. Wilson	12.3.62
Stirkeans Reenie	B	Ch. Stirkeans Astonoffs Horatio	Stirkeans Romance	Mrs E. Stirk	Mrs E. Stirk	2.4.65
Progreso Prospect	D	Ch. Progreso Lover Boy	Topsy Jane	Mr Langley	Mrs C. Hutchin	4.1.64
1967: Buranthea's Luscious Lady	B	Buranthea's Ben Braggie	Buranthea's Prime Mover	Mrs H. D. Burfield	Mrs H. D. Burfield	1.8.63

166

Name	Sex	Sire	Dam	Owner	Breeder	Date
Blairsville Tinkerbelle	B	Leodian Smart Boy	Blairsville Lady	Mr & Mrs B. Lister	Mr & Mrs B. Lister	7.9.65
Dorrit's Susanne's Treasure	B	Ch. Buranthea's Saint Malachy	Ch. My Sweet Susanne	Mrs D. Baynes	Mrs D. Baynes	10.10.65
Heavenly Blue of Wiske	D	Ch. Pagnell Peter Pan	Ch. Doone of Wiske	Mrs K. M. Renton	Mr & Mrs L. F. Palframan	28.2.63
Skyrona Blue Bobby of Streamglen	D	Ch. Skyrona Blue Prince	Enchanted Lady of Rosehara	Mrs G. Sykes	Mrs M. Waldram	3.6.65
Macstroud's Sir Gay	D	Ch. Calwyn's Wee Teddy Toff	Macstroud's Little Nell	Mr D.Stroud	Mr D.Stroud	15.1.66
Blue Flash of Streamglen	D	Wee Tich of Streamglen	Fifi Petite	Mrs Marsden	Mrs M. Waldram	3.6.65
Pagnell Blue Peter	D	Ch. Pagnell Peter Pan	Issabel Lady	Mrs D. Smith	Mrs S. I. Groom	4.4.64
Anston Lucy Locket	B	Anston Scampy Gem	Anston Sally Ann	Mrs Moore	Mrs Moore	28.9.64
Stirkean's Gerrard's Little Guy	D	Ch. Stirkean's Astonoffs Horatio	Stirkean's Polyanthus	Miss E. Thomas	Mrs E. Stirk	5.11.65

1968:

Name	Sex	Sire	Dam	Owner	Breeder	Date
Blairsville Boy Wonder	D	Leodian Smart Boy	Blairsville Lady	Mr & Mrs B. Lister	Mr & Mrs B. Lister	13.7.66
Chantmarles Mycariad Wild Silk	B	Macstroud's White-cross Dandini	Mycariad Astonoff Lady Virginia	Miss M. V. Childs	Mrs M. Hayes	16.8.66
Dandini Jim	D	Ch. Beechrise Superb	Little Enchantress	Mr B. Blamires	Mr B. Blamires	1.11.65

APPENDIX D—cont.

BRITISH YORKSHIRE TERRIER CHAMPIONS

Name of Champion	Sex	Sire	Dam	Breeder	Owner	Date of Birth
Deebees Doncella	B	Deebees Tommy Tucker	Deebees Sweet Celeste	Mr D. Beech	Mrs D. Beech	14.6.66
Luna Star of Yadnum	D	Bright Star of Yadnum	Bonny Blue of Yadnum	Mrs E. Munday	Mrs E. Munday	7.8.65
Murose Storm	D	Ch. Beechrise Superb	Murose Sherrie	Mrs E. Burton	Mrs E. Burton	21.8.66
Tolcarne Brandy Soda	D	Lamsgrove Pinnochio	Tolcarne Grenbar Kanzette	Mrs O. Wood	Mrs O. Wood	28.6.65
Whisperdales Temujin	D	Ravelin Little Jimmy	Ch. Whisperdales Phirno Carmen	Mr R. Wardill	Mr R. Wardill	8.11.66
1969:						
Bobby of Beachdale	D	Little Gay Boy of Beachdale	Janette of Beachdale	Mrs A. M. Beach	Mrs A. M. Beach	9.9.67
Chantmarles Snuff Box	B	Macstroud's White-cross Dandini	Mycariad Stargazer	Mrs M. C. Hayes	Mrs M. C. Hayes	31.10.68
Deanchel's Beau Caprice	D	Ozmilion Noble Boy	Deanchel's Sukis Blue Caprice	Mrs E. M. Taylor	Mrs E. M. Taylor	10.2.68
Deebees Gold Penny	B	Deebees Gold Plum	Ch. Deebees Little Dodo	Mrs S. D. Beech	Mrs S. D. Beech	13.2.67

168

Name	Sex	Sire	Dam	Breeder	Owner	Date
Elspeth Serenade	B	Elspeth Wonder Boy	Kelsbro Moonbeam	Miss E. Lomas & Misas P. Pass	Miss E. Lomas & Miss E. Pass	8.3.66
Macstroud's High Society	B	Ch. Macstroud's Sir Gay	Macstroud's Jacks Memory	Mr D. Stroud	Mr D. Stroud	3.1.68
Nelmila Berryfield Beauty	D	Chunky of Archombeaux	Whitecross Mitzi	Mrs I. M. Millard	Mrs I. M. Millard	10.9.64
Newholme Marco Polo	D	Wee Boy Blue	Beechrise Pixie	Mr W. K. Cherryholme	Mr W. K. Cherryholme	12.2.65
Pretty Debbie of Yadnum	B	Bright Star of Yadnum	Fair Phillipa	Mrs G. Bulgin	Miss V. E. Munday	10.12.66
Star of Keith	D	Sketrick Shi-Shi-Bu	Sketrick Sharon Rose	Mr Gardner	Mrs I. Copley	18.9.66
Tayfirs Firegift	D	Mr Teddy of Phylraine	Rosa of Recnad	Mrs J. E. Fairbrother	Mrs J. E. Fairbrother	18.8.65

1970:

Name	Sex	Sire	Dam	Breeder	Owner	Date
Blairsville Aristocrat	D	Ch. Beechrise Superb	Ch. Blairsville Tinker Bell	Mr & Mrs B. Lister	Mr & Mrs B. Lister	11.9.68
Blairsville Sherene	B	Ch. Blairsville Boy Wonder	Blairsville Belinda	Mr & Mrs B. Lister	Mr & Mrs B. Lister	29.9.67
Elspeth Nina of Ravaldene	B	Kelsbro Top Choice of Sweetloves	Elspeth Snee Susy	Miss E. Lomas & Miss E. Pass	Mr V. Ravald	1.6.67
Lyndoney Timothy Tuppence	D	Little Master of Hilfore	Lyndoney Tina Marie	Mrs E. C. Johnson	Mrs E. C. Johnson	27.6.67
Macstroud's Noble Lad	D	Ch. Macstroud's Sir Gay	Plantation Hall Susan of Wiske	Mr D. Stroud	Mrs D. Stroud	1.2.69

APPENDIX D—cont

BRITISH YORKSHIRE TERRIER CHAMPIONS

Name of Champion	Sex	Sire	Dam	Breeder	Owner	Date of Birth
Murose Wee Pippa	D	Ch. Murose Storm	Murose Blue Dawn	Mrs E. Burton	Mrs E. Burton	13.6.68
Skyrona Blue Victoria	B	Ch. Beechrise Superb	Ch. Skyrona Blue Girl	Mr Sykes	Mr Sykes	15.11.68
Super Fine of Yadnum	D	Star Superb of Yadnum	Gay Rosalinda of Yadnum	Miss V. E. Munday	Miss V. E. Munday	10.7.68
Wykebank Super Solitaire	B	Pagnell Pandarus	Wykebank Debutante	Mr B. Blamires	Mr B. Blamires	10.5.68
1971:						
Dorrit's Macstroud's Hot Toddy	D	Macstroud's White-cross Dandini	Macstroud's Mitzi	Mr D. Stroud	Mrs D. Baynes	9.1.67
Wykebank Amethyst	B	Ch. Murose Storm	Wykebank Emma Peel	Mr A. Blamires	Mr A. Blamires	28.8.68
Gaykeys Gold	D	Gaykeys Firecracker	Gaykeys Sorreldene Lucy Locket	J. & M. Hesketh	J. & M. Hesketh	19.7.68
Ravaldene Graybet Rhapsody in Blue	B	Graybet Master Mike	Graybet Blue Rose	Mr & Mrs F. L. Mitchell	Mr V. Ravald	8.9.69
Brave Warrior of Naylenor	D	Ch. Heavenly Blue of Wiske	Sombrero Daisy May	Mr P. Naylor	Mr P. Naylor	18.5.69

170

	Sex					Date
Chantmarles Bonniface	B	Macstroud's White-cross Dandini	Mydariad Stargazer	Mrs M. Hayes	Mrs M. Hayes	17.2.68
Tolcarne Drambuie	D	Ch. Tolcarne Brandy Soda	Tolcarne Blue Rain	Mrs O. Wood	Mrs O. Wood	2.12.68
Blairsville Samantha	B	Ch. Blairsville Boy Wonder	Blairsville Belinda	Mrs & Mrs B. Lister	Mr & Mrs B. Lister	5.6.70
Deebees Beebee	B	Deebees Bumble Boy	Wee Polly Fisher of Whipton	Mrs Pitcher	Mrs S. D. Beech	7.7.69

1972:

	Sex					Date
Mycariad Ragged Robin of Yadnum	D	Mycariad Tam o Shanter	Mycariad Merry Go Round	Miss M. V. Childs	Miss V. E. Munday	20.1.70
Beechrise Surprise	D	Ch. Beechrise Superb	Jane Cutler	Mrs E. Dean	Mrs H. Griffiths	2.8.70
Deanchels Prince Pericles	D	Ch. Whisperdales Temujin	Deanchels Sukis Blue Caprice	Mrs E.Taylor	Mrs E. Taylor	25.4.70
Ozmilion My Imagination	D	Ch. Blairsville Aristocrat	Ozmilion Tender Moment	Mr O. Sameja	Mr O. Sameja	14.7.70
Foxclose Little John	D	Am. Ch. Quarnhill Fuss Pot	Foxclose Blue Jean	Mrs D. M. Jackson	Mrs D. M. Jackson	22.6.70
Kellalys Miss Sophie	B	Chunky of Archambaud	Kellalys Ramleaze Mighty Atom	Mrs Kellar	Mrs Thrupp	18.4.70
Murose Exquisite	B	Ch. Murose Wee Pippa	Murose Delight	Mrs E. Burton	Mrs E. Burton	9.9.70

APPENDIX D—cont.

BRITISH YORKSHIRE TERRIER CHAMPIONS

Name of Champion	Sex	Sire	Dam	Breeder	Owner	Date of Birth
Whisperdales Deebees Halfpenny	B	Ch. Whisperdales Temujin	Ch. Deebees Gold Penny	Mrs D. Beech	Mr R. Wardill	12.5.70
1973:						
Lloyslee Lass	B	Simon Stroller	Oxcar Dinkie	Mr E. Lloyd	Mr E. Lloyd	20.4.71
Phirno Lord Gay	D	Deebee's Sunbeam	Phirno Rosie	Miss P. I. Noakes	Miss P. I. Noakes	11.4.71
Ozmilion Jubilation	D	Ch. Ozmilion My Imagination	Ozmilion Justine	Mr O. Sameja	Mr O. Sameja	4.10.71
Finstal Sugar Baby	B	Skyrona Blueboy	Streamglen Beatrice	Mrs S. Pritchard	Mrs S. Pritchard	24.2.72
Wykebank Impeccable	B	Beechrise Splendid	Wykebank Debutant	Mr A. Blamires	Mr A. Blamires	14.7.71
Macstroud's Noble Boy	D	Ch. Macstroud's Sir Gay	Chantmarles Miss Silk	Mr D. Stroud	Mr D. Stroud	4.10.71
Blairsville Most Royale	B	Ch. Whisperdales Temujin	Ch. Blairsville Shirene	Mr B. Lister	Mr B. Lister	12.5.71
Candytops Blue Peter	D	Candytops Deebee's Peter Piper	Candytops Pendora	Mr & Mrs E. H. Oakley	Mr & Mrs E. H. Oakley	3.6.71
Brascaysh Bezzer of Murose	D	Ch. Murose Wee Pippa	Macstroud's Sunshine	Mrs M. Pritchard	Mrs E. Burton	23.6.71

172

Name	Sex	Sire	Dam			Date
Chantmarles Saucebox	D	Ch. Macstrouds Sir Gay	Ch. Chantmarles Snuffbox	Mrs M. C. Hayes	Mrs M. C. Hayes	3.5.71
1974:						
Myork Muffin	D	Cartwyns Wee John	Modern Morita	Mrs K. Kemp	Mrs K. Kemp	22.10.71
Jackreed Whisky A Go Go of Stewell	D	Ravelin Little Jimmy	Jackreed Cara Tina	Mrs J. Reeder	Mrs E. Bardwell	19.8.71
Ozmilion Modesty	B	Eng. & Ir. Ch. Ozmilion Jubilation	Ozmilion Blairsville Bidene	Mr O. A. Sameja	Mr O. A. Sameja	14.4.73
Deebees Cornish Echo	D	Ch. Deebees Cock Robin	Deebees Caromias Carrissima	Mrs S. D. Beech	Mrs S. D. Beech	2.10.71
Peglea Salamander	B	Ch. Beechrise Surprise	Peglea Mon Cherie	Mrs P. Foster	Mrs P. Foster	12.9.72
Foxclose Mr Smartie	D	Ch. Foxclose Little John	Foxclose Peggy O'Neall	Mrs D. M. Jackson	Mrs D. M. Jackson	26.1.72
Chantmarles Sashbox	D	Ch. Chantmarles Saucebox	Ch. Chantmarles Bonniface	Mrs M. Hayes	Mrs M. Hayes	16.1.72
Robina Gay of Yadnum	B	Ch. Mycariad Ragged Robin of Yadnum	Gay Rosalinda of Yadnum	Miss V. E. Munday	Miss V. E. Munday	14.4.71
Kellayly's Master Tino	D	Chunky of Archambaud	Kellayly's Ramlease Mighty Atom	Mrs G. M. Kellar	Mrs G. M. Kellar	4.7.72

173

APPENDIX D—cont.

BRITISH YORKSHIRE TERRIER CHAMPIONS

Name of Champion	Sex	Sire	Dam	Breeder	Owner	Date of Birth
1975:						
Gerjoy Royal Flea	D	Ch. Beechrise Superb	Lamsgrove Missalina	Mr G. Wattam	Mr G. Wattam	9.4.71
Deebees Penny Rose	B	Ch. Deebees Cornish Echo	Ch. Deebees Gold Penny	Mrs S. D. Beech	Mrs S. D. Beech	1.7.73
Carmardy Little Henry	D	Captain Kidd	Little Lisa of Abbeydale	Mr & Mrs H. Parkin	Mrs & Mrs H. Parkin	18.4.73
Garsims Moonshine	B	Candytops Cornelius	Babette of Index	Mr & Mrs P. Rose	Mr & Mrs P. Rose	14.5.73
Macstroud's Soldier Blue	D	Eng. & Ir. Ch. Macstroud's Noble Lad	Macstroud's Society Girl	Mr D. Stroud	Mr D. Stroud	28.7.73
Clarebecks Moon Raker	D	Ch. Chantmarles Saucebox	Clarebanks Candy Mint	Mrs J. Hughes	Mrs J. Hughes	9.11.72
Naylenor Blue Monarch	D	Ch. Naylenor Brave Warrior	Wykebank Gaiety Girl	Mr P. Naylor	Mr P. Naylor	30.4.72
Lyndoney Krishna	D	Ch. Dorrit's Macstroud's Hot Toddy	Lyndoney Suzetta	Mrs D. Johnson	Mrs D. Johnson	11.11.72
Eburacum Paladin	D	Eburacum Priam	Eburacum Gem	Mr J.R. Haynes	Mrs J. R. Haynes	15.4.73

Name	Sex	Sire	Dam	Breeder	Owner	Date
Blairsville Royal Seal	D	Ch. Beechrise Surprise	Ch. Blairsville Most Royal	Mr & Mrs B. Lister	Mr & Mrs B. Lister	2.5.74
Harleta Uno Go Go	D	Ch. Whisperdales Temujin	Harleta Precious Joscelyn	Mr & Mrs Hilton	Mr & Mrs Hilton	9.5.73

1976:

Name	Sex	Sire	Dam	Breeder	Owner	Date
Empress of Murose	B	Ch. Murose Wee Pippa	Thornehowe Lady Gipsy	Mrs M. Holmes	Mrs E. Burton	2.9.74
Ozmilion Justimagine	B	Ch. Ozmilion My Imagination	Ozmilion Blairsville Bidene	Mr O. A. Sameja	Mr O. A. Sameja	3.3.75
Toy Top Tango	B	Ch. Beechrise Superb	Toy Top Topsy	Mrs D. Kitchen	Mrs D. Kitchen	8.3.73
Candytops Chantilly Lace	B	Ch. Candytops Blue Peter	Candytops Clarisa	Mr & Mrs E. H. Oakley	Mr & Mrs E. H. Oakley	30.11.73
Katie Fare of Candytops	B	Candytops Cornelius	Lanesfield Lass	Mr F. Morris	Mr & Mrs E. H. Oakley	9.2.74
Ozmilion Destiny	B	Eng. & Ir. Ch. Ozmilion Jubilation	Ozmilion Winter Goddess	Mr O. A. Sameja	Mrs J. Montgomery	26.7.74

1977:

Name	Sex	Sire	Dam	Breeder	Owner	Date
Candytops Strawberry Fare	B	Ch. Candytops Blue Peter	Sophie of Candytops	Mr & Mrs E. H. Oakley	Mr & Mrs E. H. Oakley	29.6.75
Ozmilion Distinction	D	Eng. & Ir. Ch. Ozmilion Jubilation	Ozmilion Summer Illusion	Mr O. A. Sameja	Mr O. A. Sameja	5.5.75

BRITISH YORKSHIRE TERRIER CHAMPIONS

Name of Champion	Sex	Sire	Dam	Breeder	Owner	Date of Birth
Leadmore Lady Angela	B	Leadmore Tiny Sparkle	Leadmore Blue Saphire	Mr W. Cusack	Mr W. Cusack	12.8.75
Peglea Con Tutto	D	Ch. Chantmarles Saucebox	Peglea Mon Cherie	Mrs P. Foster	Mrs P. Foster	14.11.73
Wykebank Startime	B	Ch. Blairsville Royal Seal	Wykebank Twinkle Star	Mr A. Blamires	Mr A. Blamires	12.2.76
Ozmilion Premonition	D	Ch. Ozmilion Distinction	Ch. Ozmilion Justimagine	Mr O. A. Sameja	Mr O. A. Sameja	1.8.76
Chantmarles Elegance	B	Ch. Chantmarles Saucebox	Chantmarles Nelmila Briar Rose	Mrs M. C. Hayes	Mrs M. C. Hayes	3.2.75
Ozmilion Dream Maker	B	Eng. & Ir. Ch. Ozmilion Jubilation	Ozmilion Tickle	Mr O. A. Sameja	Miss V. S. Sameja Williams	15.11.74
Craigsbank Blue Cinders	B	Southwardedge Blue	Craigsbank Sweet Kandy	Mrs J. W. Mann	Mrs J. W. Mann	30.1.76
Deebees Speculation	D	Deebees Dancing Dan	Deebees Pennys Sunshine	Mrs S. D. Beech	Mrs S. D. Beech	21.8.75
Juliette Bradstara	B	Ch. Foxclose Mr Smartie	Mistywinkle Belle	Mrs E. A. Kitching	Mr & Mrs G. Bradshaw	26.3.75

1978:

Chevawn Sweet Shonah	B	Mogid Watacharmer from Chevawn	Astolat Jasmine	Mrs J. Campion	Mrs E. Layton & Mrs S. Chiswell	28.3.76
Shaun of Beechrise	D	Speculation of Beechrise	Two Pennoth of Copper	Mrs P. Gay	Mrs H. Griffiths	29.6.75
Typros Evening Star	B	Cheeky Boy of Typros	Macstrouds Evening Star	Mrs Da Silva	Mrs Da Silva	17.1.74
Verolian Justajule with Ozmilion	D	Eng. & Ir. Ch. Ozmilion Jubilation	Ozmilion Wild Temptress	Miss V. Sameja Williams	Miss V. Sameja Williams	28.2.76
Ozmilion Exaggeration	B	Ch. Ozmilion My Imagination	Eng. & Ir. Ch. Ozmilion Modesty	Mr O. A. Sameja	Mr O. A. Sameja	13.9.76
Wellshim Madam of Deebees	B	Deebees Oberon	Dainty Dinah of Wellshim	Mrs A. C. Shimwell	Mrs S. D. Beech & Mrs A. C. Shimwell	25.12.75
Typros the Devil of Spicebox	D	Chantmarles Spice Box	Snowdrop of Typros	Mrs Da Silva	Mrs Da Silva	14.7.75
Naylenor Magic Moment	B	Naylenor Battle Cry	Naylenor Honey Bunny	Mr P. Naylor	Mr P. Naylor	3.12.76
Blairsville Royal Warrant	D	Ch. Beechrise Surprise	Ch. Blairsville Most Royal	Mr & Mrs B. Lister	Mr & Mrs B. Lister	13.11.76
Jackreed Apple Blossom	D	Jackreed Jiminy Cricket	Mistress Emma of Jackreed	Mrs J. Reader	Mrs J. Reader	25.3.76

177

APPENDIX D—cont.

BRITISH YORKSHIRE TERRIER CHAMPIONS

Name of Champion	Sex	Sire	Dam	Breeder	Owner	Date of Birth
1979:						
Fascination of Daisydell	D	Daisydell Midsummer Lad	Miss Tina of Heymor	G. Taylor & Miss S. Moreli	Mrs J. Turner	23.3.77
Chantmarles Stowaway	D	Chantmarles Tartar Sauce	Chantmarles Caress	Mrs M. C. Hayes	Mrs M. C. Hayes	18.4.76
Harletas Ferdinando	D	Evenwood Ambassador	Chantmarles Miss Rosebud	Mrs L. Hilton	Mrs L. Hilton	12.3.76
Chantmarles Debutant	B	Chantmarles Tartar Sauce	Chantmarles Nelmila Briar Rose	Mrs M. C. Hayes	Mr P. Boot	8.8.76
Carmardy Marcus	D	Captain Kydd of Carmardy	Cinderella of Parkabbey	Mr & Mrs H. Parkin	Mr & Mrs H. Parkin	1.3.77
Ozmilion Tradition	D	Ch. Ozmilion Premonition	Ch. Ozmilion Exaggeration	Mr O. A. Sameja	Mr O. A. Sameja	1.1.78
Wykebank Wild Rose	B	Ch. Blairsville Royal Seal	Wykebank Twinkle Star	Mr A. Blamires	Mrs K. I. Henderson	12.2.76
Candytops Raffles	D	Ch. Candytops Blue Peter	Melody Fare of Candytops	Mr & Mrs E. H. Oakley	Mr & Mrs E. H. Oakley	12.11.76

178

Name	Sex	Sire	Dam			Date
Deebees My Fascination	D	Deebees Dancing Dan	Ch. Wellshim Madam of Deebees	Mrs S. D. Beech	Mrs S. D. Beech & Mrs A. C. Shimwell	17.5.77
Ozmilion Heart's Desire	B	Ch. Ozmilion Premonition	Ozmilion Justaromance	Mr O. A. Sameja	Mr O. A. Sameja	3.1.78
Chantmarles Dolly Dimple	B	Ch. Chantmarles Stowaway	Chantmarles Maggie May	Mrs M. C. Hayes	Mrs M. C. Hayes	3.6.77
Beechrise Sweet Solitaire	B	Ch. Swank of Beechrise	Sundae of Beechrise	Mrs H. Griffiths	Mr & Mrs D. Sargison	13.10.76
1980:						
Daisydell Tinker	D	Daisydell Midsummer Lad	Daisydell Spring Juill	Mr & Mrs W. Keen	Mrs J. Turner	24.8.77
Murose Illustrious	D	Eburacum Pimento Murose	Murose Merry Go Round	Mrs E. Burton	Mrs E. Burton	15.11.76
Craigsbank Miss Dior	B	South Wardedge Blue Spark of Craigsbank	Craigsbank Sweet Nanette	Mrs J. W. Mann	Mrs J. W. Mann	10.9.77
Ozmilion Devotion	D	Ch. Ozmilion Premonition	Ch. Ozmilion Justimagine	Mr O. A. Sameja	Mr O. A. Sameja	5.6.78
Chantmarles Proper Madam	B	Ch. Chantmarles Stowaway	Chantmarles Inis Cara	Mrs M. C. Hayes	Mrs M. C. Hayes	7.5.78
Souvenir of Beechrise	D	Ch. Shaun of Beechrise	Coletts Cheeky Debbie	Mrs M. Cole	Mrs H. Griffiths	16.10.77

APPENDIX D—cont.

BRITISH YORKSHIRE TERRIER CHAMPIONS

Name of Champion	Sex	Sire	Dam	Breeder	Owner	Date of Birth
Wykebank Tinkerbell	B	Blairsville Royal Monarch	Wykebank Vanity Fair	Mr A. Blamires	Mr A. Blamires	24.2.78
Deebees Golden Delight	B	Deebees Othello	Barlizsue Eee Emma	Mrs S. D. Beech & Mrs A. C. Shimwell	Mrs S. D. Beech & Mrs A. Shimwell	27.7.78
Blairsville Gaiety Boy	D	Blairsville Royal Monarch	Blairsville Dream Girl	Mr & Mrs B. Lister	Mr & Mrs B. Lister	5.10.78
Candytops Candyman	D	Ch. Candytops Blue Peter	Candytops Florence	Mr & Mrs E. H. Oakley	Mr & Mrs E. H. Oakley	3.12.77
Ozmilion Ovation	D	Ch. Ozmilion Tradition	Ch. Ozmilion Heart's Desire	Mr O. A. Sameja	Mr O. A. Sameja	11.1.79
Mogid Millionairess	B	Ch. Ozmilion Premonition	Mogid Just Dolly	Mrs M. Giddings	Mrs M. Giddings	1.9.77
1981:						
Johnalenas Silken Charm	D	Ch. Ozmilion Distinction	Nelmila Berryfield Justine	Mrs K. E. John	Mrs K. E. John	30.10.78
Ozmilion Story of Romance	B	Ch. Ozmilion Devotion	Ch. Ozmilion Exaggeration	Mr O. A. Sameja	Mr O. A. Sameja	25.6.79

Name	Sex	Sire	Dam			Date
Finstal Johnathan	D	Garsims Captain Moonshine	Finstal Evita	Mrs S. Pritchard	Mrs S. Pritchard	9.3.79
Marshonia Blue Secret	D	Marshonia Inspiration	Marshonia Love Story	Mrs P. Robinson	Mrs P. Robinson	3.5.79
Candytops Fare Delight	B	Ch. Candytops Cavalcadia	Ch. Katie Fare of Candytops	Mr & Mrs E. H. Oakley	Mr & Mrs E. H. Oakley	10.5.79
Summer Sensation of Sedae	B	Ch. Ozmilion Distinction	Mitu Pito of Kumar	Miss E. Silva	Mrs M. Eades	10.5.79
Murose Masterpiece	D	Ch. Murose Illustrious	Madam Murose	Mrs E. Burton	Mrs E. Burton	29.9.79
Franbrin Royal Sapphire of Woodcross	B	Franbrin Royal Admiral	Chiqueta of Vandepere	Mrs F. Thorley	Mrs J. Mills	14.3.78
Chandas Shonah's Girl	B	Ch. Ozmilion Distinction	Ch. Chevawn Sweet Shonah	Mrs E. Layton & Mrs S. Chiswell	Mrs E. Layton & Mrs S. Chiswell	19.11.78
Candytops Cavalcadia	D	Ch. Blairsville Royal Seal	Candytops Chantilly Lace	Mr & Mrs E. H. Oakley	Mr & Mrs E. H. Oakley	15.9.77
Chantmarles Rose Bowl	B	Ch. Chantmarles Sauce Box	Chantmarles Isadora	Mrs M. C. Hayes	Mrs M. C. Hayes	22.6.75
Chantmarles Celebrity	D	Ch. & Ir. Ch. Ozmilion Jubilation	Chantmarles Maggie May	Mrs M. C. Hayes	Mrs M. C. Hayes	2.10.80

1982:

Name	Sex	Sire	Dam			Date
Stewell Moonstorm	D	Jackreed Whiskey-a-go-go of Stewell	Alvin Cindy Mae of Stewell	Mrs E. Bardwell	Mrs E. Bardwell	24.6.79

BRITISH YORKSHIRE TERRIER CHAMPIONS

Name of Champion	Sex	Sire	Dam	Breeder	Owner	Date of Birth
Shipps Shanty Man	D	Drummer Boy of Shipps	Ships Truly Fair	Mrs D. M. Hamill	Mrs D. M.Hamill	2.7.80
Relation of Prime Meadow's	D	Prime Meadow's Sophist	Branshole Peppe	Mrs Wright	Mrs I. Robson	2.7.80
Ozmilion Flames of Desire	B	Eng. & Ir. Ch. Ozmilion Jubilation	Ch. Ozmilion Exaggeration	Mr O. A. Sameja	Mr O. A. Sameja	12.1.81
Wykebank Star Choice	B	Wykebank Wonder Boy	Wykebank Starshine	Mr A. Blamires	Mr A. Blamires	27.9.79
Chantmarles Best Intentions	D	Eng. & Ir. Ch. Ozmilion Jubilation	Ch. Chantmarles Dolly Dimple	Mrs M. C. Hayes	Mrs M. C. Hayes	7.11.80
Ozmilion Expectation	D	Ch. Ozmilion Ovation	Ch. Ozmilion Story of Romance	Mr O. A. Sameja	Mr O. A. Sameja	14.7.80
Moseville Misty Lady of Hankeyville	B	Star of Beechrise	Golden Madonna	Mrs M. Tracey	Mrs J. Handforth	12.7.80
Deebees Dominic	D	Deebees Oberon	Quiberon Dominique	Mrs S. D. Beech & Mrs A. C. Shimwell	Mrs S. D. Beech & Mrs A. C. Shimwell	9.10.80

Ozmilion Flames of Passion	B	Ch. Ozmilion Ovation	Ch. Ozmilion Destiny	Mr O. A. Sameja	Mr O. A. Sameja	5.11.80
Sharwin's Easter Dream	B	Ch. Ozmilion Distinction	Bopeep of Sharwin	Mr & Mrs D. M. Baldwin	Mr & Mrs D. M. Baldwin	15.4.79
Jamesson's Royal Stewart	D	Ch. Blairsville Royal Seal	Jamesson's Blue Fascination	Mr & Mrs J. Henderson	Mr & Mrs J. Henderson	18.4.80
Verolian Temptress with Ozmilion	B	Eng. & Ir. Ch. Ozmilion Jubilation	Ozmilion Lovestory	Mrs V. M. Sameja-Hilliard	Mrs V. M. Sameja-Hilliard	18.9.80
Wenwyte Whisper's Boy	D	Ch. Candytops Cavalcadia	Wenwytes Winter Whisper	Mrs W. F. White	Mrs W. F. White	24.4.80
Chantmarles Wild Rose	B	Ch. Foxclose Mr Smartie	Chantmarles Isadora	Mrs M. C. Hayes	Mrs D. M. Lorenz	28.10.78
1983:						
Kindonia Justin	D	Ch. & Ir. Ch. Ozmilion Jubilation	Kindonia Premier Girl	Mr & Mrs G. Briddon	Mr & Mrs G. Briddon	25.2.81
Mondamin My Minstrele	B	Ch. Ozmilion Tradition	Mondamin Endeavour	Mrs I. Dawson	Mrs I. Dawson	25.4.80
Craigsbank Stormy Affair	B	Craigsbank Sirius	Craigsbank Stephanie	Mrs Mann	Mrs J. Leslie	20.2.80
Ozmilion Love Romance	B	Ch. Ozmilion Tradition	Ch. Ozmilion Heart's Desire	Mr O. A. Sameja	Mr O. A. Sameja	3.4.81

BRITISH YORKSHIRE TERRIER CHAMPIONS

Name of Champion	Sex	Sire	Dam	Breeder	Owner	Date of Birth
Arlestrey Regal Challenge	D	Ch. Blairsville Royal Seal	Arlestrey Memoire Cherie	Mrs E. Howarth	Mrs E. Howarth	23.9.79
Beebeemi Blaze	B	Ch. Blairsville Royal Seal	Heidi of Peppinoville of Beebeemi	Mr & Mrs Mitchell	Mr & Mrs Mitchell	11.5.79
Ozmilion Dance of Romance	B	Ch. & Ir. Ch. Ozmilion Jubilation	Ch. Ozmilion Story of Romance	Mr O. A. Sameja	Mr O. A. Sameja	29.7.81
Ozmilion Invitation	D	Ch. Ozmilion Expectation	Ch. Ozmilion Exaggeration	Mr O. A. Sameja	Mr O. A. Sameja	20.2.82
Candytops Royal Cascade	D	Ch. Candytops Cavalcadia	Candytops Ribbons Delight	Mr & Mrs E. H. Oakley	Mr & Mrs E. H. Oakley	1.10.81
Azurene Moss Rose of Yadnum	B	Yadnum Star Touch	Yadnum Love Joy of Azurene	Mrs I. G. Bulgin	Miss V. E. Munday	26.5.80
1984:						
Emotions of Ozmilion at Rosamie	D	Ch. Swank of Beechrise	Minetown Bluebell	Mrs J. Handforth	Mr J. Magri	9.11.81
Typros Royal Splendour	D	Ch. Swank of Beechrise	Typros Rewarded at Last	Mrs G. Da Silva	Mrs G. Da Silva	29.10.81

184

Coletts Charmain	B	Ch. Ozmilion Ovation	Coletts Princess	Mrs M. Cole	Mrs M. Cole	1.2.82
Naejekim Blue Reflection	D	Naejekim Blue Flint	Naejekim Anita	M. W. Bebbington	Mrs E. Carr	20.11.81
Stewell Soul Singer	B	Stewell Sensation	Stewell Tinkerbelle	Mrs E. & Mr & Mrs S. Bardwell	Mrs E. & Mr & Mrs S. Bardwell	27.5.81
Evening Blue	D	Naejekim Blue Flint	Blairsville Sue Ellen	Mr & Mrs K. Gillespie	Mr & Mrs K. Gillespie	5.6.82
Blairsville Royal Pardon	B	Blairsville Royal Monarch	Blairsville Royal Destiny	Mr & Mrs B. Lister	Mr & Mrs K. Gillespie	22.9.81
Chantmarles Candy	B	Ch. Chantmarles Stowaway	Chantmarles Bella Paula	Mrs M. C. Hayes	Mrs M. Hayhthorn-thwaite	2.10.79

1985:

Maritoys Midnight Rose	B	Lyndoney Little Cracker of Maritoys	Jerin's Briar Rose of Maritoys	Mrs M. Watton	Mrs J. M. Blamires	17.3.83
Naylenor Crown Jewel	D	Ch. Candytops Cavalcadia	Naylenor Regal Rose	Mr P. L. Naylor	Mr P. L. Naylor	18.8.82
Ozmilion Hopelessly in Love	B	Ch. Ozmilion Distinction	Ch. Ozmilion Flames of Desire	Mr O. A. Sameja	Mr O. A. Sameja	6.4.83
Azurene Corduroy of Yadnum	D	Yadnum Star Touch	Yadnum Love Joy of Azurene	Mrs I. G. Bulgin	Miss V. E. Munday	23.7.81
Taurusdale Pilihan Hati	D	Kellaylys Master Tristram	Taurusdale Tender Touch	Mr D. Kee	Mr D. Kee	1.7.82

APPENDIX D—cont.

BRITISH YORKSHIRE TERRIER CHAMPIONS

Name of Champion	Sex	Sire	Dam	Breeder	Owner	Date of Birth
Craigsbank Sheeza Lady	B	Craigsbank King of Hearts	Craigsbank Romance	Mrs J. W. Mann	Mrs J. Leslie	1.6.82
Yadnum Regal Fare	D	Ch. Candytops Cavalcadia	Yadnum Love Joy of Azurene	Miss V. E. Munday	Miss V. E. Munday	2.4.83
Marshonia Secret Serenade	B	Marshonia Startrek	Marshonia Love Affair	Mrs P. Robinson	Mrs P. Robinson	3.6.83
Marshonia Top Secret	D	Ch. Marshonia Blue Secret	Marshonia My Precious Clare	Mrs P. Robinson	Mrs S. Parker	29.11.80
Carmardy Cassius	D	Ch. Ozmilion Expectation	Carmardy Angelena	Mrs J. Parkin	Mrs J. Parkin	20.11.83
Verolian Appreciation at Ozmilion	D	Ch. Ozmilion Distinction	Verolian Theme on a Dream at Ozmilion	Mrs V. Sameja-Hilliard	Mrs V. Sameja-Hilliard	12.9.82
1986:						
Polliam Sweet Delight	B	Eng. & Ir. Champion Ozmilion Jubilation	Polliam Sweet Destiny	Mrs P. Osborne	Mrs P. Osborne	5.7.82
Ozmilion Kisses of Fire	B	Ch. Ozmilion Expectation	Ch. Ozmilion Heart's Desire	Mr O. A. Sameja	Mr O. A. Sameja	1.8.84

186

Shianda Royal Fanfare	D	Deebees Othello	Shianda Cara Cree	Mr & Mrs J. G. Davies	Mr & Mrs J. G. Davies	18.1.83
Keriwell Flirtation	D	Eng. & Ir. Ch. Ozmilion Jubilation	Karina Mine	Mr J. E. Wells	Mr J. E. Wells	10.9.83
Christmas Fable	B	Ch. Ozmilion Distinction	Fatal Charm	Mr & Mrs K. Gillespie	Mr & Mrs K. Gillespie	16.12.83
Ozmilion Admiration	D	Ch. Ozmilion Invitation	Ch. Ozmilion Love Romance	Mr O. A. Sameja	Mr O. A. Sameja	24.8.83
Chandas Inspiration	D	Ch. Ozmilion Invitation	Ch. Chevawn Sweet Shonah	Mesdames E. M. Layton & S. Chiswell	Mesdames E. M. Layton & S. Chiswell	3.1.84
Lovejoy's Debonnaire Dandy	D	Arlestrey Haydons Majestic	Bevmells Lavender Blue	Mrs S. P. Schaefer	Mrs S. P. Schaefer	30.4.82
Lena Alanah Snowdrop of Cyndahl	B	Chozebar Solara	Anna Bella Sunshine	Mrs Sears	Mrs E. J. Morris	10.2.82
Ozmilion Dedication	D	Ch. Ozmilion Admiration	Ch. Ozmilion Heart's Desire	Mr O. A. Sameja	Mr O. A. Sameja	29.4.85
Candytops Royal Sovereign	D	Ch. Candytops Royal Cascade	Candytops Lady Levant	Mr & Mrs E. H. Oakley	Mr & Mrs E. H. Oakley	20.8.83
Meadpark Silk n' Velvet	B	Meadpark Personality Plus	Meadpark Blue Blaize	Mr & Mrs R. Mulligan	Mr & Mrs R. Mulligan	19.8.84
Verolian the Adventuress at Ozmilion	B	Ch. Verolian Justajule with Ozmilion	Verolian the Seductress at Ozmilion	Mrs V. M. Sameja-Hilliard	Mrs V. M. Sameja-Hilliard	21.1.85

INDEX

Page numbers in *italic* refer to the illustrations